Is modern first-class cricket too serious for the players to enjoy? Ray East doesn't think so. He is blessed with an instinct for seeing the funny side of things, and his spontaneous humour has lit up grounds all over the cricketing world. Now the joker of the county circuit has provided accounts of some of the most amusing episodes from his long career both in county cricket and on tours abroad. Opponents, umpires, colleagues and captains all provide the raw material for his stories, and he is quite able to see a joke against himself.

After a promising schoolboy cricketing career, Ray East began an apprenticeship as an electrician and played village cricket for East Bergholt, Suffolk. He was spotted by a former Essex player who arranged for him to have a trial with the County. He made progress into the county side, gained his county cap in 1967 and was thought by many judges to be unlucky not to have won international recognition. He took part in his county's great triumphs – the Championship and Benson and Hedges Cup in 1979, and John Player League in 1981.

A FUNNY TURN

Confessions of a Cricketing Clown

A Funny Turn

Confessions of a Cricketing Clown

RAY EAST

Written in association with Ralph Dellor

Illustrated by Bill Tidy

London
UNWIN PAPERBACKS
Boston　　　　　Sydney

First published in Great Britain by George Allen & Unwin 1983
First published by Unwin Paperbacks 1984
Reprinted 1984

UNWIN® PAPERBACKS
40 Museum Street, London WC1A 1LU, UK

Unwin Paperbacks
Park Lane, Hemel Hempstead, Herts HP2 4TE, UK

George Allen & Unwin Australia Pty Ltd
8 Napier Street, North Sydney, NSW 2060, Australia

Text © Ray East and Ralph Dellor, 1983
Illustrations © Bill Tidy, 1983

British Library Cataloguing in Publication Data

East, Ray
  A funny turn.
  1. Cricket
  I. Title II. Dellor, Ralph III. Tidy, Bill
  796.35'8'0924   GV917
  ISBN 0-04-796086-8

Set in Garamond by Inforum Ltd, Portsmouth
and printed in Great Britain by Cox & Wyman Ltd, Reading

Contents

CHAPTER ONE

Running In

'Cricket's a funny old game.' I think every player, reporter and commentator ever connected with cricket has resorted to that phrase at some time or another. I suppose I have been credited, or accused, with helping to bring out the comical element in the game more often than most, and I must admit that I do enjoy seeing the funny side and at the same time giving some harmless entertainment to the spectators. They tend to regard my antics in one of two ways: for every ten spectators who are amused when my humour manifests itself on the field there is always one who is heard to suggest that if only I would stop playing the fool and get on with the game I would be a much better cricketer. I am reminded of the high-handicap golfer who followed two air-shots by excavating an enormous divot from the fairway. He turned to his caddy and said, 'Golf's a funny old game' (for it is also an eminently adaptable phrase!) to which his dour, very Scottish caddy replied, ' 'Tis nae meant to be.'

The fact is that any humorous incident which does occur is entirely spontaneous and is not planned as a comedy routine. I see some other players larking about but realise they must have been sitting in the pavilion working out what they are going to do to amuse the crowd. I am not that sort of person because my natural inhibitions – and I do have plenty – would not let me act like that. It would be as unnatural for me to go out of my way to try and be funny as it would for me to try curtailing my humour. It either just happens as a matter of course or it doesn't happen at all.

To give an example which should prove the point, I can remember playing against Surrey at Ilford in 1972. Their opening batsman, Michael Edwards, was going through a bad patch. He had scored just 4 in the first innings and was doggedly summoning up all his powers of concentration in an attempt to stay there and block his way back into form. Apart from Edwards having trouble, the 'Troubles' in Ireland had reached a pretty warm stage and I am married to an Irish girl, Barbara. I was bowling to Edwards and just as I got to my delivery stride, a car back-fired sharply in the road which runs alongside the ground. Instead of going through with the delivery I threw my arms into the air, let out a pained groan and fell to the ground as if shot. The crowd and players looked aghast for a moment as they thought I must have become the first left-arm spinner to fall victim to a sniper's bullet in the middle of an over! Then everyone realised what had happened and the laughter rang out as clearly as had the car's report. All the players were convulsed – apart from Michael Edwards as he tried to repair his shattered concentration. I replied to his glares with an apology but there was no way that I had been trying to put him off. I could not have pre-meditated that scenario, but the comic in me just refused to let the opportunity for mirth pass by. Furthermore, it hardly affected the course of the match for Edwards went on to gather 34, yet the crowd had enjoyed a light-hearted moment in an otherwise serious contest between bat and ball.

There have been several critics over the years who have voiced the opinion that incidents like this reflect an uncaring attitude towards the game. They say that if only I took it seriously, I could have played for England. I suppose the selectors might have taken a similar view for, with all

modesty, I don't think I would have been the worst player ever to appear for his country if I had received the nod. I might not have been good enough to make a big impact in Test cricket but had I ever been given the chance, my commitment would not have been found wanting. My behaviour might not always find favour with the most serious-minded of establishment figures but it has never threatened to cause an international incident.

People might think that I do not take cricket as seriously as such a game deserves, but I would refute that opinion. While my left arm is travelling along the course from which it delivers the ball, I am taking the game just as seriously as, for instance, Geoff Boycott when he is batting: I would rate my concentration at the critical moments no lower than that yardstick. The difference is that whereas some people find it impossible to maintain their concentration other than in a continuous pattern, I can switch on and off at will and so my effectiveness as a cricketer is in no way impaired when I crack a joke in between balls. I am not alone in this. I have heard Colin Milburn, the burly Northamptonshire and England batsman, start to tell a joke to the close fielders, break off long enough to hit a superb boundary, and then deliver the punch-line with all the panache he had used to dismiss the ball to the ropes. He was a big, cheerful man whose appearance was totally in keeping with his character. He was told that he would be a better batsman if he could shed a few dozen pounds or so but it did not work that way. There was a seventeen-stone character in a fourteen-stone body and it was not a happy match. I am sure it would be the same if I tried to change my character. I do not think the mask of tragedy could be comfortably worn by this clown.

To me cricket has always been a game to be enjoyed and I have retained that same attitude throughout my career. It began in very modest circumstances. I was born at Manningtree in Essex but lived in a little village just over the Suffolk border called East Bergholt. It was there, at school, that I first played cricket and it was also there that I played my first village match. I was just 11 years old at the time and in the time-honoured tradition was called into the team to play with my father, a wicket-keeper, and uncle when they were one man short. I remember my debut quite clearly. East Bergholt were playing a team called Ipswich Greyhounds and managed to amass a total of 11! I went in last to face the last ball of an over from their pacy opening bowler, who went back to his full run. There I was, peering in trepidation over the top of borrowed pads as this ogre came tearing in. Before he reached the wicket, however, my Uncle Les, who was the other batsman, stepped across into the bowler's path and I heard him asking in no uncertain terms what he thought he was doing. Now Uncle Les was a big man and the bowler agreed to lob the ball down from a couple of paces. I missed the ball, the ball missed the stumps, and Uncle Les duly missed the first ball of the next over and was bowled, thus sparing me from further embarrassment.

I could have done with Uncle Les at the other end in 1970 at Ilford when Essex were playing Lancashire. Ken Shuttleworth was running through us on a flyer and none of the Essex batsmen was relishing one of his faster spells. When it came to my turn to face the flak I made my way from the pavilion towards the vacant wicket — and then straight on past it to join the non-striker. I leaned nonchalantly on my bat alongside the other batsman, looking at the other end. That brought forth a ripple of appreciative laughter, but what happened next reduced everyone on the field to helpless mirth. Before going to take up my proper position I called to the impatient bowler, suggesting that my courage was no match for his pace. 'Well pitched up on middle and off will do me, Shutt' were the words I used to open negotiations for the purchase of one cheap wicket. The Lancashire fielders, who had clearly heard this exchange, prepared to avoid the flying splinters of my wicket as Shuttleworth came roaring in and put one on the spot just as ordered. To his horror, instead of seeing me allow the ball to hit the wicket, he watched me cream the half-volley through the covers for four. The fielders enjoyed that, but Shuttleworth was absolutely furious. He stood at the end of his follow-through, hands on hips, glaring at me with total venom, and if there was not steam snorting from his nostrils there could have been. Eventually he turned and stomped back to his mark, occasionally casting thunderous looks over his shoulder in my direction. Now I have always considered that I have a fairly shrewd cricketing brain and I did not need to tax it to guess what was coming next. As his arm came whistling over I jettisoned my bat and dived out towards point. I landed, flat out, well in time to look up and see the ball bouncing at great pace some six feet above me. When the fielders had recovered from their bout of hysteria they told me it was the only time they had seen the usually taciturn Ken Shuttleworth grin all season. Between them, Uncle Les and my humour have stood me in good stead against fast bowlers!

After my village debut I started to play regularly on both Saturdays and Sundays and I remember when I was 13 taking 8 for 21 on a trip into Essex to play a side from near Clacton. Batsmen at that level were not only unable to see my chinaman coming, they did not even realise what had happened after it had hit the stumps. I continued to find success when I moved up in standard to play respectable club cricket for Brantham. That team was good enough to boast a couple of Suffolk players in its ranks, and to have an annual fixture against a team raised by Peter Smith, the former Essex and England leg-spinner. It seems that I made an impression on him for he arranged that I should have a trial with the county at the start of the next season.

I was invited to go along to a net session at Fairlop early in March, so I took time off from my work as an apprentice electrician to attend. My father also took a day off and Peter Smith himself gave us a lift from home to the ground. He could not stay to watch, however, and having left us at the gate went off to keep a business appointment. Dad and I stood around waiting for something to happen but nothing did, so eventually I gingerly made my way into the pavilion to change. I went into the home dressing room to be told by Gordon Barker in his native Yorkshire tones, almost unintelligible to my Suffolk ears, that the room was for the 1st XI players and not for the likes of me. Then I went next door to the room marked 'Away Team' to be greeted by Graham Saville's Cockney message to the effect that I could not change in the room reserved for 2nd XI players. I changed in the corridor between the two.

I bowled and bowled in the nets, trying all I knew to impress, while the capped players treated nets as they always did – an excuse to see how far they could hit the ball. Dad went off to chase the ball for me, and I went on wheeling away for all of two hours. Eventually they got bored with it, nets came to an end and I went back to my corridor to change. Nothing was said, nobody offered either friendship or advice, and it was not until we were making our way out of the gates to go home that Trevor Bailey caught up with us. Not knowing whether to expect a fat contract or the big heave-ho I waited, only to find that the county captain dealt with my eager anticipation as carefully as he might have faced the new ball from Lindwall and Miller. 'We'll be in touch,' he said, adding Cantabrigian to a growing collection of accents.

For three months I heard nothing, and then suddenly I was asked to report to the Dagenham Cables ground to play for the 2nd XI against Worcestershire. My mother immediately

15

got out her knitting needles and began to knit me a new sweater, using a pattern which included more heavy ribbing than is usually found on a North Sea fisherman's jersey. Complete with this, now my pride and joy, my canvas boots and skinny trousers, I arrived at the ground to be greeted by the skipper, county coach Frank Rist. When I was changed, Frank took one look at me and enquired, 'What have we got here?' Singling out my new sweater for particular attention, he asked if it was the only one I had. The boots and trousers he would accept. He did not even raise an objection to the Suffolk Schools cap which topped the ensemble. But the sweater had to go. Generously he gave me one of his own and, while the gesture was appreciated, it could not be mistaken for a perfect fit. Frank was a big man in every respect while at that time, though tall, I had to run around in the shower to get wet. I took the field looking like a badly erected bell-tent.

The Worcestershire team was a strong one, captained by Joe Lister and including experienced players like Ted Hemsley and Doug Slade. In the first innings I really did feel how I looked – the country boy from Suffolk – but I picked up a couple of wickets and then got six in the second innings. Then came a game against Somerset 2nd XI with the likes of Mervyn Kitchen and Graham Burgess, when I again picked up wickets. In three games with the Seconds I took 20 cheap wickets and then the call came; I was to report to the Gallows Corner ground in Romford where the 1st XI had a match against Oxford University.

You could hardly blame the gateman for refusing me admission to the ground without paying. I had my kit in a canvas hold-all and carried my bat in my hand. I did not have any pads of my own. I had arrived early and when I said I was an Essex player, the guardian of the ground gave me a highly suspicious look. I often think that there should have been a

17

last line of defence during the war after the men at the front and the Home Guard. It would have been made up entirely of the more officious breed of cricket steward. If Hitler had tried to invade these shores he would have been met by a short, stout man in a white coat who would have undoubtedly said, 'I don't care who you are, you're not coming in here unless you're a member!'

Not without difficulty I managed to get to the Essex dressing room, and no wonder I was nicknamed 'Dick-Dick' by the other players, for I must have looked like a character straight out of a Dickens novel. I stood in wonder, gazing at the plush leather cricket bags arrayed along the seats. MCC touring colours abounded and, still clutching my hold-all and bat, I read the names: Trevor Bailey, Barry Knight, Brian Taylor. I tried to find an inconspicuous corner, only to be told that spot was reserved and I would have to find somewhere else. It was like the trial all over again.

16 June 1965 was a wet day and I wondered what the twelfth man had to do under such circumstances, for I was sure that would be my lot. But Trevor Bailey introduced me to the rest of the team and told me I was in the XI. Only two hours play were possible that day and I took one of the three wickets to fall while the University scored 55. On the second day, *Wisden* recorded, 'the left-arm spin of East and the leg-breaks of Hobbs ended the innings for the addition of another 53 runs.' I finished with 3 for 28 from 15 overs and took another wicket for 17 in ten second-innings overs. Set to score 73 in 46 minutes, we won by four wickets off the penultimate ball with one R.E. East next on the card.

My most vivid memory of those three days in June 1965 was the way the other members of the team occupied their time when not batting. Some slept, even with pads on while waiting to go in. Others read, played cards or did the crossword. I had always played cricket in a team where every

member of the company watched every ball, and all this extraneous activity appeared very strange to me. I can still see in my mind's eye Trevor Bailey at his typewriter in the middle of the dressing room, tapping out an article for a newspaper or magazine, while Graham Saville, never short of a word or two hundred, stood by the window giving what amounted to a ball-by-ball commentary. Nothing he said could attract the captain's attention until Keith Fletcher went in. The news that Michael Bear had hit four went unregarded. So did his dismissal. Fletcher's first run had Bailey lifting his eyes to the ceiling and waxing lyrical about his protegé's batting ability and his future as an England batsman. The thought that I might reach such heights did not come within a million miles of my thinking at that time. Whichever way my career, such as it was then, went in the future, I had already reached a significant landmark: I was a county cricketer.

CHAPTER TWO

To Cap it All

I did not get another first-team game during 1965 and divided my time between playing cricket for my club and the county 2nd XI, and working as an apprentice electrician. The firm were very good about giving me time off to play mid-week fixtures but before the start of the 1966 season I had to make a decision about my future. I was offered a contract worth the staggering amoung of £260 to join the Essex staff for the coming campaign. Now there are some lads who set out with nothing else in mind but to be professional sports-men, so when they are given such an opportunity at the age of 16 their only decision is which club to join. My problem was that I had not grown up with this one aim in life, as I had never really believed myself to be good enough. Further-more, any ambitions I had towards a career in professional sport tended to centre on Ipswich Town Football Club rather than Essex County Cricket Club.

This was too good a chance to miss, however, and despite my father's misgivings, I decided to have a crack at cricket. My reasoning was that I could spend a year finding out if I was likely to make the grade and if things did not work out, I could go back to being an electrician. So I signed on the dotted line and made my way back to Fairlop for some more pre-season training, this time as a professional. The press were there, and my mother still has the photograph of me being greeted by a wellington-boot-shod Trevor Bailey as I arrived for my first day as a professional cricketer.

There is a popular theory that as soon as a cricketer dons whites and goes out onto the field the heavens open. This is not strictly true. Cricketers will tell you that when they report back for pre-season training there will be a biting east wind, gusting from strong to gale force, usually laced with a little cold rain or sleet in much the same way as a cook might add salt to taste. The ball smacks into frozen hands, shoulder joints creak beneath every sweater that can be found, and any sudden movement on a soggy outfield sends you skidding towards a hefty cleaner's bill without too many marks for artistic impression or technical merit. Gradually, as the start of the season gets closer, the weather improves, only to revert to form for the opening week of matches.

It was conditions like those, windy and bitterly cold, that in 1981 caused our opening match against Cambridge University at Fenner's to be halted. Despite a colourful array of clothing not usually associated with cricket, like scarves and bobble hats, the umpires decided that it was really too cold and so play was suspended. I had been fielding at deep fine leg with little to do in the way of running about to keep warm and nothing to do in the way of bowling. So I borrowed an overcoat from the scoreboard operator and expressed my view about the suitability of the temperature for cricket by taking the field wearing it!

When training began at Fairlop I could have been excused for thinking that my footballing ambitions had been fulfilled. Fitness training consisted of lengthy games of soccer between the capped and uncapped players. Matches lasted for as long as it took the capped players to win. Whatever time was left was devoted to nets, conducted with varying degrees of seriousness and always with an awful lot of bowling for R.E. East. Coaching was minimal: Frank Rist was a lovable

character but did not believe in some of the more scientific theories about instruction. His main contribution was to put his arm round my shoulder and say, 'Come and have a cup of tea, son.'

There are some rather pukka cricket sides whose captains report back to the management about the suitability of triallists for full club membership. These reports contain details not only about cricketing abilities but also about table manners at tea. I can only presume that I behaved with sufficient decorum while drinking the numerous cups of tea Frank Rist invited me to consume, and that my cricket was coming along to the required standard, because in May 1966 I got the call to play in my first County Championship match. It was not going to be an easy baptism for we were to play Warwickshire, a side packed with class batsmen, on a flat Edgbaston pitch.

The adventure started for me even before the match itself began. First there was the journey. It was not too difficult a journey when compared with an astronaut's visit to the far side of the moon, but for the still-yokel East, there was little to choose between them. By now I had become the proud owner of a proper cricket bag, although my initial enthusiasm for it wore a little thin after lugging it to the bus stop in the village, then trying to cope with it on the lurching, crowded, four-mile trip into Manningtree to catch a train to where I could pick up a lift for Birmingham. I did not make many friends but could have influenced a few people with whom I, or my cricket bag, came into contact.

Staying in a hotel was something else new to me. In later years on the county cricket circuit I have got more used to hotel life than I might want, but back in 1966 it was a case of watching what everyone else did and trying not to be too conspicuous in following their example. My other abiding memory of my debut was the socialising which went on between the two teams. I was used to the odd beer or two with opponents but I found that in county cricket the two sides were almost indistinguishable off the field. Everybody knew everyone else and the match seemed to provide the excuse for an old boys' reunion only interrupted by the cricket. I did not only meet the opposing players either. There I was, a country swede, chatting over drinks in the committee room with the Warwickshire chairman. If it had been club cricket I think we would have been lucky to retain the fixture!

There was plenty of time to socialise, for rain prevented any play until after tea on the second day. When we did get going Warwickshire batted first and rattled up 92 for 1 declared. I contributed nine runs to their collection from the only over I bowled, before being spared the doubtful privilege of batting when Essex declared with two wickets down having just passed the Warwickshire total. I spent the next morning chasing around the outfield as the Warwickshire batsmen went all out for the victory which they were ultimately to achieve. Neal Abberley hammered an undefeated 117, while it was an England captain and a fine player of spin-bowling, M.J.K. Smith, who was the other batsman in full flight when I came on to bowl just after lunch. Trevor Bailey set a conventional six-three off-side field for me and I responded with a reasonable line. The only trouble was that the batsmen responded by reaching outside the line and lapping me through mid-wicket. I kept glancing over to our captain, who showed no inclination to change the field to meet the circumstances which prevailed, so eventually I plucked up the courage to suggest that a reinforcement of the leg-side field might cut off a few boundaries. The reply came that MJK might make a mistake. He made no mistake, lapping his way to 43 not out while I conceded 37 runs from nine overs without claiming my first Championship wicket.

Needing 215 to win, we were losing wickets yet getting close enough to the target to ensure that I would have to bat and if I could hold an end up, someone else might be able to scrape together the winning runs. Those were the visions of grandeur I enjoyed as I made my way from the pavilion gate to the middle to face the England opening bowler, David Brown. He had seemed a nice enough chap when socialising but as he waited at the end of his run his humour must have temporarily deserted him. I took guard and looked around the field before settling into my stance. That was the signal for the bowler to begin his approach. Now I had heard of David Brown tractors, and with all due respect to a very fine bowler, what was coming towards me at a fearsome rate looked for all the world like a piece of agricultural machinery with a mind of its own. On he came, arms pumping as he gathered pace, until he reached the wicket and exploded into a blur of flailing limbs. I felt that such a display of flamboyant aggression should be met with a calm defensive shot which I duly executed. I think they were still looking for the off bail when I got back to the pavilion to find my colleagues guffawing merrily. I failed to understand why they were so cheerful when I had done nothing to further the team's cause. The fact of the matter was that I had not reached the top of my back-lift when the ball sent the off stump cartwheeling back, and there was nothing these professionals enjoyed more than watching one of their brotherhood exposing the failings of someone yet to measure up to the standards required. They saw that as the height of amusement; I had seen nothing and the match was lost by 24 runs.

It was in another match that season R.E. East, cricket comedian, first made an appearance. We were playing Yorkshire at Bradford and I contributed just three of the 65 overs which Yorkshire needed to run up a total of 263 for 8. Between innings Fred Trueman came into our dressing room to introduce himself to those he had not encountered before. After asking the names of one or two less well-known members of our side and mentally totting up his haul, he came to me. 'And who have we got here?' he enquired.

'Raymond East,' I replied, trying to disguise the tremors in my voice.

'Dear, oh dear,' intoned Fred with a dismissive chuckle, and then, glancing round at the assembled company as if to make sure he had left nobody out, 'I can see six or seven wickets in this room, oh yes, six or seven for FST today.'

He was not far wrong, though for once a little on the conservative side, for he managed 8 for 37, including me for one.

I did not bowl in their second innings, but I had plenty of fielding to do down at fine leg. There is an incline to the Park Avenue ground which meant that I was slightly above the level of the pitch and there was a tendency to send my returns over the top of wicket-keeper Brian Taylor. The crowd enjoyed that, and even Trevor Bailey was laughing as 'Tonker' Taylor got more and more upset at the throws going whistling over his head. Eventually I got the range worked out and sent in an accurate throw. The crowd cheered sarcastically and I responded by raising my cap in acknowledgement. Always ready to accept a bit of by-play, the crowd laughed and I found myself enjoying the laughter. My natural humour had been released and suddenly I felt at home and at ease.

Not that it was laughter all the way from then on. In fact, looking back, 1966 could feature quite prominently among the contenders as the most worrying year of my life. Having made the decision to play full-time cricket, I had appeared in 13 matches in the first part of the season. During them I had not bowled very much and had certainly not set the Thames alight with my performances. My 12 wickets had cost 40 each and when the university term ended my place in the side was taken by David Acfield. I saw what appeared to be the old school tie being knotted in a noose around my neck. Here was the village cricketer being ignored in favour of a Cambridge Blue. However slim my contribution had been during those 13 matches, and however well 'Ackers' performed in the matches that followed, I could only take a biassed view.

I did get a first-team summons later that year and it was delivered in the manner of most summonses – by the police. On this occasion I was pleased to see the uniformed officer at the door of our telephone-less house, informing me that Essex had put out an SOS for me to get to Taunton as injuries had depleted their travelling party. Some years later I was not so pleased to encounter the constabulary when driving home some time after the close of play. I was having a little trouble with the handbrake when along came an officer, enquiring if I needed any help. He got into the car to find what was causing the problem, yanked the offending piece of machinery in an attempt to free it, and was left looking a little sheepish as the handbrake came away in his hand. In retrospect I think I rather overplayed the part of the indignant innocent: 'Oh that's nice, isn't it? Can I be of assistance, sir, he says and then wrenches my handbrake off with his bare hands. That's very helpful, that is.' It was then that the policeman caught a whiff of my breath and I said goodbye to my driving licence.

Back in 1966 I did not have a licence to lose. It was a case of getting my kit together and, as quickly as the public transport system would allow, getting myself the 250 miles from East Anglia to the West Country. This involved crossing London, so I armed myself with an underground map and, for only the fourth time in my life, went exploring in the big bad city. Not that I saw much of it, for I disappeared down onto the Circle Line at Liverpool Street, emerged again at Paddington, and was whisked away towards the setting sun. The sun had well and truly set when I eventually reached the hotel at one o'clock the next morning. I had enjoyed visions of being greeted by a grateful captain who would thank me for making an effort to get there and for coming to the team's aid in its hour of need. He would attend to my every comfort and enquire which end I thought would suit me best the next morning. Reality was a little different. There was nobody waiting to greet me for they were all in bed, and I had to find my own way to a room with no sort of refreshment.

It was at breakfast that I learned of the injuries which had beset the party. Brian Taylor had chipped a finger during the previous match at Worcester but had played and kept wicket despite the injury. Furthermore he was going to play again with it in Taunton. Another chipped finger belonged to leg-spinner Robin Hobbs, so it seemed obvious that he would now be able to drop out and I could maintain the complement of spinners. We all went off to the ground, I got changed and went out for fielding practice, and it was not until I returned to the pavilion that I found out without being told directly that Robin was going to play and that I had raced through the night and across England to be twelfth man.

The irony of it all was that I had to play an active part in the match despite the fact that I had been designated as the drinks waiter. Somerset batted first and in the sixth over of the morning, opening bowler Tony Jorden, later to become an England rugby player, chased a ball to the boundary and tried to cut it off by stepping on it and flicking it back just short of the line. He did get a foot on it, but instead of a piece of athletic fielding he managed only to help the ball over the rope while at the same time turning his ankle. This prevented him from taking any further part in that innings or the Somerset second innings, so I spent most of the three days on

the field without being able to bowl as Somerset cantered to a 101-run victory. They were three days which did not exactly have me falling about appreciating what a funny old game cricket is.

The journey to Taunton had given me the opportunity to do some thinking. I had been acutely aware that the time was approaching when I would be told whether I was to be retained for the following season or not, and I saw this match as giving me the chance to press my claims at the last knocking. I cannot think that my performance as twelfth man against Somerset could have tipped the scales one way or the other, but it was not long after that I was told to stop worrying for I was being offered another contract. I responded by establishing myself in the side, and I took 61 wickets in 1967. It seemed to me that I had justified the club's decision to keep me on the staff and my own step in pursuing a career in county cricket. By the end of 1967 a major change had been forced upon me. I had to leave off my Suffolk Schools cap; instead I was awarded one by Essex.

Even that ceremony, the major highlight of a county cricketer's career, did not pass off without incident in my case. We had just finished a County Championship match and I had gone into the bar for a drink. Strangely enough, I was with Keith Boyce, just idly chatting about the match we had completed and half-listening to the results from elsewhere on a nearby radio. I had mentally switched off after the last result when my attention was wrenched back once more by the line '. . . and the news has just come in that Keith Boyce and Ray East of Essex have been awarded their county caps.' It appears that the secretary, Major 'Topper' Brown, had made an announcement to the press without thinking to check whether anyone had mentioned the fact to Boycie and me. I believe I arrived a little earlier than usual next morning, warmly lapping up the congratulations from members and colleagues, until Tonker Taylor, who had taken over from Trevor Bailey as captain, decided the moment was right to make a gracious presentation. There was perhaps a slight lack of pomp and dignity as he delivered the citation. His exact words were: 'Right, here we are then. The rest of the world seems to know about it already so you'd better have the bloody things. Well done.'

CHAPTER THREE

Trevor, Tonker and the Gnome

Brian Taylor was my second county captain, and he played a major part in my development. I am not sure whether it was because of my lack of years and experience that I had not struck up an immediate, warm kinship with Trevor Bailey, my first captain, but I tended to find him rather distant and uncommunicative. Maybe I held him in too much awe ever to get close to him, for he was already a legendary figure in the game when I began watching him, let alone playing under him. As a boy I had regularly gone along to watch Essex play at Colchester, and Bailey was the man who always stood out in the Essex side. He and Doug Insole would invariably wear their MCC touring sweaters with a blaze of red, yellow and blue in bands around the neck and waist, while the other members of the team only had the three scimitars adorning the front of their sweaters.

In terms of ability, too, it seemed to me that Trevor Bailey stood out considerably from the others. At times it even appeared that there was Bailey and ten others representing Essex. When I was a teenager I had been a tearaway fast bowler, rushing in and frightening out batsmen by the length of my run. It was obvious that Trevor Bailey had figured prominently among heroes to be worshipped, not only by me but by nearly every Essex schoolboy of the time. In many an East Anglian household meal-times were punctuated by a father imploring his son to eat his greens or he would never be able to play cricket like Trevor Bailey. The difference in my case was that I might not play like him, but I was playing with him.

There was no doubting that he had an immense knowledge about the game, as is evident when you hear him talk about it now, but at the end of a long and distinguished career he perhaps lacked the commitment to apply that cricketing brain to the task in hand. Rather than dominating the course of a match, he tended to let it evolve on its own. That was as a captain. As a player he still showed signs of the great cricketer he had been, and the youngsters in the side like me had to marvel at the way he answered the physical demands of the game.

Seeing Trevor Bailey prepare for a session in the field was like a lecture in anatomy. Various unreliable parts of his body were strapped up, often to more durable parts if there were any available in the vicinity. The end result, swathed in bandages, looked like an Egyptian mummy. That structure would be covered with his whites and the whole ensemble finished with two or three MCC sweaters. The wonder was not that he could bowl so well once warmed up, but that he could bowl at all.

Even at this time of life he was the master of swing and cut. Given favourable conditions, his control of the ball found out all but the most technically correct batsmen. That was once he was loose; getting loose took time. His favourite ploy in this was the practice run. It might not have been strictly within the regulations to run up to the wicket two or three times without actually delivering the ball, but Trevor managed it. 'Sorry, batsman,' he would shout in an irritated voice, 'lost my run.' Then back to his mark, turn, and along measured strides that he could have hit with his eyes shut he came again, only to halt after a few strides to repair a wayward boot-lace. '*So* sorry, batsman' would be the enhanced apology this time, before he made his way once more back to his mark. Eventually, like the pilot of an aircraft with a misfiring engine at the end of a runway, he would be satisfied that all cylinders were firing and he would set off down a smooth run before gathering himself into a lovely high action. The first few looseners might go anywhere, but he seldom strayed in line or length from then on.

I remember one such day at Ilford when Essex were playing Somerset. It was in May 1966 and the first time there had been Sunday play in a County Championship match. Barry Knight and Tony Jorden opened that attack in Somerset's second innings and, by the time Trevor considered it right to bowl himself, there were quite a few runs on the board. He had to strike the right balance between warming up and wearing himself out before turning his arm over, and on this occasion he did not quite prepare enough. Geoff Clayton, a diminutive wicket-keeper who had moved to Somerset from Lancashire, was facing as Trevor came gliding up to the wicket for his first ball. It was a slow long hop which Clayton had every intention of dispatching into the next parish. There was a look of murderous glee in the batsman's eyes and a groan of dismay from the bowler as the ball went cracking off the bat towards square leg. It was on the boundary in those far distant regions of Ilford that Robin Hobbs, a superb fielder, grasped the ball out of the air with both hands just as it was due to end its life as a six. Clayton could not believe he was out; Bailey offered the most casual of confident congratulations to his accomplice.

It was as a batsman with an impregnable defence that Trevor Bailey assumed legendary proportions. 'The Barnacle' had broken many a bowler's heart, causing him to wonder if the Bailey bat being thrust forward to check his best delivery really conformed to the regulations concerning width. In Australia he defied Lindwall and Miller at their peak by resolute defence against the lifting ball. Never one to miss a psychological trick, he would test Keith Miller's temper to its limits by going back to deal with a lifter, dropping it at his feet, and then peering round from behind his bat with an impish grin on his face.

Christopher Martin-Jenkins, in his *Who's Who of Test Cricketers*, compares Trevor Bailey's all-round abilities and comes to the conclusion that he was better to watch as a bowler than as a batsman. For the general public that might have been the case, but I can remember an instance when I was delighted to watch him bat. We were playing a Derbyshire side which included Harold Rhodes, who was as fast as anyone around at the time. The initial movement of most of our batsmen, facing a very hostile Rhodes on a pitch of totally unpredictable bounce, was neither backwards nor forwards — it threatened the well-being of the square-leg umpire. Trevor, however, showed just what a gutsy cricketer he was by moving onto the front foot. He was given a fearful battering but stayed there, and I was more than happy to watch it all from the pavilion.

When the captaincy moved to Brian Taylor in 1967, the county's fortunes were at a low ebb and we professionals realised that we were not employed by the most secure organisation in the world. The bank balance was usually printed in one of the club's colours, red, and there were precious few assets around. One advantage, although it might not have appeared so at the time, was that we had a good crop of younger players who could develop together. The other was the appointment of Brian Taylor as captain. He in fact got the job in front of the senior professional, Gordon Barker. Gordon was a little Yorkshireman who, day in, day out, was one of the most consistent opening batsmen in county cricket. He scored some 20,000 runs for Essex and was unlucky never to have played for England. Mind you, I dread to think what sort of state he would have got into had he been selected. There is a story, and a perfectly true one, that he was left at 98 not out overnight at Trent Bridge against Nottinghamshire and was found at six o'clock the next morning walking round and round the outfield. He had not been able to sleep for worrying over those extra two runs and could find no other way to fill in the time until the start of play. If you asked him about it now, he would not only be able to tell you how he scored those two runs when play did start, but could recall exactly how he got the other 98. Come to think of it, if you have inexhaustible patience and a couple of weeks to spare, he could probably talk you through most of his first-class runs.

Despite that fine record and his seniority in the side, it was decided that Brian Taylor, our wicket-keeper, was the man to take over from Trevor Bailey. Apart from the change of captaincy there was also a change in administrative attitude off the field. To keep the county going, overheads were trimmed to the barest minimum and the playing staff slashed from 22 professionals to a mere 11, one of whom was a reserve wicket-keeper, Rodney Cass. The playing strength was supplemented by David Acfield when he was on vacation from Cambridge University, and by a few amateurs brought in from club cricket to make up the numbers. It was often said that we played attractive, positive cricket in those days because we would go into the field with three spinners in our ranks. The fact was that we rarely had any alternative.

I sometimes wonder why we needed to have two wicket-keepers on the books when Brian Taylor was one of them. Between 1961 and 1972 he played in 301 consecutive Championship matches and missed just one other match

during that time. Such was his durability that he would play on with chipped fingers, pulls, strains and anything else. We were playing Surrey at the Oval one day and Robin Hobbs took a wicket with a leg-break which hit the top of the off stump. The bail flew up and caught Tonker just above the eye, causing quite a nasty gash. Keith Fletcher, surveying the blood flowing freely from the injury, suggested that he went off for some treatment, but he would hear nothing about it. 'Just a little nick,' Tonker insisted, dabbing it vigorously with the back of his gauntlet and making even more of a mess. Eventually, with blood streaming down his face and all over his whites, he was persuaded to leave the field for treatment. Such was his reputation as a hard man that the batsman at the other end, Stewart Storey, watched him go past and then asked, 'Where's he going – to get a staple put in it?'

Tonker could be something of a medical man himself. When I first came into the side I tended to suffer from the odd bout of cramp. Dr Taylor knew a remedy for that, of course. I would be sitting down to eat my lunch when an iron grip would take hold of my shoulder and my ears would be assaulted by brusque, sergeant-majorish tones: 'Got a bit of cramp out there, did we, son? Salt deficiency causes that, you know. I never suffer from it. I have plenty of salt on my food.' And with that he would lean over, take the salt cellar and deposit most of its contents over my lunch, rendering it inedible. He was quite right in that I did not suffer as much cramp afterwards, or perhaps it was just that I did not notice it as much because I was so hungry.

That sort of treatment was relatively harmless. What he once prescribed for Graham Saville was potentially rather more dangerous. We were playing Worcestershire at Chelmsford and Graham had tried to hook a short ball from Brian Brain. Instead of four past square leg he got a top edge

39

and the ball crunched into his mouth. He did not even bother to come off the pitch towards the pavilion but went in exactly the opposite direction, to get treatment in the local hospital on the far side of the Chelmsford ground. 'There's nothing wrong with him, he'll be OK,' barked Tonker as Graham disappeared towards the casualty department, or even intensive care for all we knew.

Some time later we saw a white-clad figure, specked with scarlet, making uncertain progress round the ground towards the pavilion, half-carried by two medical orderlies. When Graham got to the pavilion he looked dreadful. He was pale, he could hardly stand unsupported and his mouth, from which two teeth were missing, was swollen, bruised and bloodied.

'How do you feel?' enquired our captain with what was, for him, surprisingly tender concern.

'Not too bad' appeared to be the reply mumbled weakly by the patient.

'That's the spirit, Graham, good. Now what I always reckon is when you get a little knock, get straight back out there, so I want you to go back in next wicket down.'

Now batsmen have been known to be carried off the field on a stretcher, but not many arrive at the wicket by that means of transport. That would have been about the only way Graham Saville could have covered the ground from pavilion to middle at that moment, but it took a great deal of persuasion before Tonker agreed that he was in no fit state to continue.

It is very easy to overlook the contribution Brian Taylor made to Essex cricket at this time. He was just the right type of man to lead a young, inexperienced team and a proportion of the credit for the successes in later years must be given to him. A nucleus of the side which won the Benson and Hedges Cup and County Championship in 1979 and the John Player

League in 1981 learned its cricket under Brian Taylor. Several times we came close to giving him the opportunity to lift a trophy aloft in triumph but we could not quite manage it. At the time he was captain and I was playing under him we frequently did not see eye to eye. There was something of a generation gap between us and at that stage of my career I could not appreciate that a disciplinarian was needed to pull the team together.

If I did not always understand Brian Taylor, Brian Taylor certainly did not always understand me. A cheerful man with a ready grin, he was always pretty serious about his cricket and was more than a little suspicious of my activities. I remember playing against Northamptonshire one day when the sun was beating down, Mushtaq Mohammad had one ton and looked set for another, and Northants had over 200 for 2 on a typically flat, lifeless pitch. None of our bowlers could get anything out of it, least of all me. I had been plugging away for some 20 overs without a hint of encouragement when suddenly, in the last over before tea, a ball took off. For some reason a ball pitching on the leg stump turned side-ways, giving neither the batsman nor Tonker the slightest chance of making contact, and it went for four byes. Graham Saville ran to retrieve it, and when he got back to occupy the solitary slip position he found Tonker muttering to himself. He was apparently saying, 'He turned that one deliberately just to make me look a fool!' It was a case of suspicion getting the better of reason, for I would not have bothered to bowl 20 overs without turning one ball just to create the chance of tricking the skipper.

Brian Taylor had been brought up in an age when wicket-keepers were not expected to stand up to medium-pacers and above, and he was quite competent at accepting chances which came to him standing back. In a side which now employed three spinners he had problems. He could usually get something in the way to stop the ball, but without too many frills. For instance, most wicket-keepers at the first-class level spend hours breaking in a new pair of gloves before they would dream of wearing them in a match. They hammer them and work them until they are as supple as the proverbial kid gloves. They will have them made to measure so that they become almost a second skin, which is why you will see some Test keepers with what appear to be a tatty old pair: they become so attached to them thay cannot bear to part with them.

Tonker subscribed to a different school of thought. He liked to be immaculate in appearance, and that went for his gloves too. I have actually seen him come into the dressing room, take a brand-new pair of wicket-keeping gloves out of a plastic bag and, with a few words of admiration for their condition, go out and use them in a match. They would be so stiff that he had a job to bend his fingers round the ball in them and they were about as supple as dinner plates. I always got the impression that he had to balance the ball on them rather than letting it go into the cup. I envied left-arm spinners like Derek Underwood having a 'keeper of the calibre of Alan Knott behind the stumps, and Derek himself once got a taste of my problems.

He was playing for T.N. Pearce's XI, with Tonker keeping wicket, during the Scarborough Festival one year. The pitch looked as if it might be the sort on which 'Deadly' could earn his nickname, and so the captain gave him the ball and set the field. Derek came plodding in to bowl in that splay-footed way of his, and the first ball was very much a loosener, humming down the leg-side for four byes with Tonker no-where. The next one pitched leg, turned and lifted to beat the bat and hit a surprised Tonker high on the right shoulder. 'Derek,' he shouted down the pitch, 'you're meant to be a world-class bowler, so you see these gloves – you'd better hit them 'cos they're not f—ing moving.'

Having said that, Brian Taylor was a more than useful county cricketer at the peak of his career, and he very nearly went one better than that. He went on the MCC tour of South Africa in 1956–57 without getting a Test, and that was the winter after he had been voted the Best Young Cricketer of the Year. As a hard-hitting no. 3 left-handed batsman he once scored over 1800 runs in a season and passed the 1000 mark eight times, while his best season behind the stumps gave him 91 victims. As a tactician, one of his greatest assets was that he would take advice from Keith Fletcher. I sometimes felt that Keith was running the side a long time before he was eventually appointed county captain.

Tonker finally gave up the captaincy in 1974 after putting the county back on its feet. He left Keith the basis of a fine side which eventually tasted success in 1979. I had been friends with Keith Fletcher from the time I first joined the staff. We were both country boys and I had often stayed with his parents after matches when I had been unable to make the tortuous journey back to my own home, while the entry in the scorebook recording my very first wicket in first-class cricket read 'c Fletcher b East'. I helped to spread the use of his nickname – 'The Gnome'. That originated at the time when pointed shoes had almost gone out of fashion, but Fletch still wore a scuffed old pair on which the toes actually turned up. He came into the changing room wearing them one day and looked as if he had just fallen off a toadstool.

I have an enormous respect for his ability as a captain and I thought it a tragedy when the England selectors discarded him after he had led the side through India and Sri Lanka. If I do have a criticism of his captaincy it is that he perhaps shows a little too much bias to seam bowling; David Acfield counters what he sees as this dogmatic inflexibility by referring to Keith as 'Adolf', but when the ball is turning we get our chance. Then he expects the spinners to do their stuff and I sometimes get the impression that he expects more from me than anyone as we have been mates for so long.

When he was sacked from the England job it must have been a great comfort to him to go around the country with Essex and get genuine sympathy from professionals wherever he went. They all knew that he was still the best skipper around. I have heard it suggested that he lacks courage against fast bowling, but that is a total fallacy. Nobody relishes the really quick men, but he has a better technique to deal with it than most and has the record to prove it. Further, I will refute any hint of cowardice on his part when he is prepared to stand as close to the bat at silly point as he does for me. There have been times when even I have thought him foolish, and it is not often a bowler will admit to that when there is a chance of picking up wickets. I can remember getting wickets, too, thanks to his willingness to field there. At Worcester in 1967, on a near-perfect batting wicket, Tom Graveney had just come in and I had to bowl to him knowing that if I strayed off line or length he was likely to stroke me away through the covers elegantly and effortlessly. I do not know whether it was Fletch's idea or Tonker's, but he certainly agreed to go in close at silly point, showing rather more confidence in my ability to keep it on the spot than I had myself. Furthermore, the ploy worked. Tom stepped back to give himself room to stroke a ball wide of the fielder but he got a little too far back on his stumps, knocking all three over as he played the shot. Perhaps the entry in the scorebook should have read 'pressurised Fletcher, 1' instead of 'hit wicket, b. East, 1'. Either way, Tom cannot have been too happy in missing out on a big score, for his partner at the time, Basil d'Oliveira, went on to amass the little matter of 156.

For all that we have been close friends over the years, Fletch and I do not have the same sense of humour. This has sometimes got me into trouble and once caused me to be disciplined and dropped from the team. We were playing once more on one of those Northampton wickets where a real lifter can sometimes get stump-high. It was in 1980, the year after our Championship and Benson and Hedges successes, and we were suffering something of a reaction. On this day we were struggling to hold on for a draw after having a go for the runs and losing wickets, and I was facing little Richard Williams bowling his off-breaks. Now he is all of five foot six tall, and I should think the top six inches of that is his curly hair. I was battling away as hard as anyone, but with the ball keeping so low I allowed myself to play one forward defensive shot going down on one knee as if about to be knighted. It was not a knighthood I received some three overs later when I got back to the pavilion after being bowled by Jim Griffiths. I was accused of not trying and setting a bad example, the row became more and more heated, and it only ended when I packed my bag and walked out.

Because we had been such close friends it was not easy to apologise, and I went four matches without having any contact with the club. In the end I had to admit that it had been a silly thing to do, leaving myself open to accusations of throwing my wicket away. On his part Fletch conceded that he had been a little hasty and I was forgiven. Now we are as close as ever again and we all appreciate his leadership in Essex even if the England selectors do not. I sometimes wonder if his rather shy, retiring nature counted against him in the job. While others might go seeking the headlines it has always appeared that he is ill-equipped to become a strong media personality. It is not his fault, it is just the way fate has dealt out the cards, but it is a little unfortunate that a man who cannot sound his 'r's' spent years driving a red Capri!

Apart from a fine side, Keith Fletcher seems to have inherited Brian Taylor's indestructability. Since he was made captain he has missed few matches, so the rest of us seldom get a chance to lead the side. Graham Gooch has occasionally done so, and Keith Boyce tried his hand at the job too. I was never entirely happy about Keith's appreciation of the tactics required, for he was essentially an inspirational cricketer rather than a leader. I remember playing with him at Leicester in the first year the 20-overs-in-the-last-hour ruling was operational. We were trying to play out the ten remaining overs with Keith Boyce facing Ray Illingworth, and the rest of us in the pavilion could not believe what we saw. There was Keith, dancing down the track and sweeping a six. The next ball he tried to do the same again, but Illy was a little too clever for him and had him stumped. I was the next man in and as we crossed just outside the pavilion gate, I asked Keith what he was trying to do, playing extravagant shots like that with just ten overs to go and no hope of winning. 'Well, man,' he replied, 'I thought that if I could hit the ball a long way out of the ground it would take them more time to get it back.' And that was when there would be another ten overs however long they took!

I have also had the honour of captaining the side occasionally, and had the thrill of doing so when the Australians toured England in 1981. Rod Marsh was leading them and helped to make it a memorable match. There has always been a special atmosphere between Essex and the Australians since they took 721 off our attack in just one day at Southend in 1948. Consequently there was a huge crowd at Chelmsford despite very heavy overnight rain. The umpires, Arthur Jepson and Peter Eele, decided that the ground was strictly unfit for play, but we could go out if we wanted to keep the spectators happy. Despite the fact that the fifth Test was less than a week away and there was always the chance of somebody falling awkwardly or pulling something, Rod Marsh agreed that we should, in his words, 'give it a go', so play started half an hour after lunch. We had a very good match too, with the Australians going into the last innings needing 247 to win. They lost early wickets so that at one stage they were still 138 behind with half the side out. Then Wood and Yallop put on 94 in just 75 minutes but I kept the game open, bowling myself and David Acfield, and they finished ten runs short with only two wickets standing.

I had also skippered the side at Derby earlier in 1981 in a match that, even by my standards, was not without its fair share of incident. To begin with, three batsmen managed to record all-run fives in their scores without the aid of overthrows. Then, during the match, it was announced that Bob Taylor, the Derbyshire and England wicket-keeper, had been awarded the MBE in the Queen's Birthday Honours list. It was too good an opportunity to miss and as Bob made his way to the wicket the whole Essex team lined up along his path and dropped to one knee in mock homage. We did not worry to pay the same respect when he was out for two a few minutes later, caught off my bowling.

That was also the match in which we made a little bit of cricketing history by having a substitute captaining the side, much to the dismay of the umpires. Keith Fletcher had been injured and was unable to take his place in the team on the first day, a Saturday, but had more or less recovered by Monday. When we were in the field and needed a substitute it was he who came on, and he immediately started to take control. That was just before the tea interval, during which umpire David Evans came over and said that it was not allowed for the captain to be outside the nominated 11 players, as detailed in the very first paragraph of the Laws of Cricket. So after tea we went back into the field and I took with me a piece of paper. Whenever I was setting the field or making a bowling change, I would ostentatiously take out what was in fact a blank sheet of paper and studiously consult

49

it, pretending that Fletch had put it all down in writing for me before we went out again. Fletch played along with it all and we got a nice little routine going whereby I would try to move him and he would either stay where he was, giving meaningful looks with which I would hurriedly concur, or even move in the opposite direction. David Evans himself has a lovely sense of humour and he was quick to appreciate that he was getting sent up something rotten, but he accepted it all in a perfect spirit. After all, can't umpires, and captains, enjoy the game too?

CHAPTER FOUR

Close Call

Playing under people like Trevor Bailey, Brian Taylor and Keith Fletcher has given me a pretty good insight into three very different types of captaincy. Each has had his own style and approach to the game, but my experience of skippers has not been confined to those leading Essex. Over the years I have been on tours and played in sides captained by a rich variety of characters, among them several men who have been called upon to lead the England Test team. When playing under one of them, Ray Illingworth, I had high hopes that I might be able to bowl myself into the England team.

I was in his side, flatteringly labelled 'The Rest', in the 1973 Test trial against the England team which had toured India the previous winter. This was the first time for many years that such a trial match had been arranged and my hopes of the event leading to greater things for me were justified by the fact that only two men playing for the Rest did not represent their country – M.J. Smith of Middlesex and me. Ray Illingworth was one of the best tacticians I have ever played under and I thought that his shrewd cricketing brain, allied to the fact that he too was a spin-bowler and so understood our problems, might help me along a little bit in such exalted company. As things turned out it was a little bit of luck rather than any predetermined planning which gave me a prominent position in the records of those three days at Hove in 1973.

Graham Roope of Surrey, who had made his Test debut the previous winter, decided that he could secure his place in the side for the coming series against New Zealand by a big score in the trial. Furthermore, he appeared to have picked me out as the bowler off whom he was going to get his runs. My 15.3 overs had cost 56 runs when Roope, with 117 to his name, tried to drive me for another four. The ball was intercepted on its way to the boundary by a diving David Lloyd at extra cover, who held onto an amazing catch. The next man in was another Surrey player, Pat Pocock. 'Percy', as he is always known, is never likely to challenge for an all-rounder's spot, but he does take his batting very seriously. There is a story in cricket that he wore glasses to bat in for the first time when Surrey played Middlesex at Lord's. He arrived at the wicket looking very intent and studious, much to the delight of the Middlesex fielders. Wicket-keeper John Murray gave him a particularly hard time. 'What have you got those on for, Perc?' he asked.

'So I can hear better,' replied Percy sarcastically as he prepared to face his first ball from Fred Titmus.

It was a flighted yorker which he had to dig out amidst clouds of dust, only to receive the barbed comment from behind the stumps, 'You didn't hear that one too well, did you?'

Apparently Percy was not hearing the ball too well at Hove, for the first one I bowled to him found his pad in front and the umpire's finger aloft. 2 for 56 looked a little better with one ball of my sixteenth over to go and the last man, Bob Cottam, coming to the crease. As is customary when a bowler is on a hat-trick, the fielders clustered around the bat with all the self-restraint of vultures ending a fast. At such a time a cricket pitch is a very lonely place to be. The batsman has the added pressure of trying to prevent the deed, while the bowler knows that he does not get too many opportunities to achieve it in his career. Those avaricious close fielders, outwardly eager for a catch, are deep down afraid that they might grass a chance that does come their way and so ruin the big moment. Even the umpire knows the importance of the decision he might be called upon to give.

In this instance the umpire did not have a difficult decision to give, and when the ball flew off Bob Cottam's bat, David Lloyd made no mistake with the catch. I had completed the first and only hat-trick of my career. Naturally I was delighted with the achievement and thought that it might just be spectacular enough to catch the selectorial eye. I was rooming with John Lever and he too could be satisfied with his day's work: 2 for 16 off his 13 overs represented an excellent piece of bowling at that level. We were both rather buoyant next morning when we went down to breakfast and the lift stopped on the way to let in Alec Bedser. By the time we had got to the ground floor that mood of expectancy had totally evaporated as the chairman of selectors greeted us with a 'Good morning, Roy. Good morning, Peter.' If we had made so little impression that he did not even know our names, what chance did we have of making the team?

The next time I knew I was at least under consideration for the England side was twelve months later when there was another Test trial, this time at Worcester. On this occasion I was playing under Tony Lewis without really understanding what the selectors were trying to find out. That view was confirmed by John Snow, who walked into our dressing room before the start to meet his colleagues in the team labelled 'The Rest' asking, 'What am I doing here?' He said it without malice but with simple mystification, and not without reason when you consider that at the time he had some 1000 wickets to his credit in first-class cricket and was sixth in the list of English Test wicket-takers with 176.

Tony Lewis was not a dynamic leader and his style of

captaincy was not ideally suited to get the best out of John Snow. The latter was in one of his introspective moods, bowling at little above medium pace towards the end of the second day. I was fielding at mid-off and suggested that he might like to show us a really quick over to round off the day. Poor Dennis Amiss was batting, and I use the word 'poor' advisedly for he was unaware of what was about to hit him. He had been confidently playing Snowy off the front foot and looking world-class when suddenly the storm broke. From having all the time in the world to play his shots he found himself facing the first five balls of the last over of the day with all the calm composure of a man fleeing a rampaging bull. They were the quickest deliveries we had seen in the match, and Dennis was fending them off his chest. By complete contrast Snow bowled the last ball off a four-yard run, a slow off-break which was gratefully despatched to the boundary.

John Snow was a difficult man to handle and understand, as was confirmed when we both went to South Africa in 1973–74 with Derrick Robins' XI under Brian Close. He bowled quite magnificently on that tour but ran into a bit of disciplinary trouble, as he was wont to throughout his career. As an established Test player he did not perhaps attach the same importance to the tour as he might have when playing for England, but there was no lack of effort on the field, where we relied very heavily on him as the spearhead of the attack. After one little clash with the tour leadership during the day before the last of the three four-day representative matches against the South African XI in Johannesburg, he was late for the team meeting that evening. When he did not arrive it was thought that he was acting up over the previous incident, so I was sent to find him. The bar came to mind as a likely place to start and sure enough, he was there enjoying a quiet drink with a friend. He did not appear over-impressed by my mission, we stayed for another a quick one, and John was dropped from the team. On the whole, the tour management came out of that conflict rather worse than he did, for without his penetration in the attack the South African batsmen ran riot. Eddie Barlow smashed a double-century, Lee Irvine, who had been an Essex player for a time, also took a century off the depleted bowling, and the South Africans rattled up 528 for 8 before declaring and going on to win by an innings and 83 runs with a day to spare.

Even without that drink in the bar I would not have been involved in that match. In fact it was a mystery to me why they had bothered to ask me along, for I played very little cricket at all. On the entire trip I bowled just nine overs in first-class matches, and while it was all very pleasant to enjoy a two-month paid holiday in the sun, I could have got so much more out of it. Several players have enhanced their reputations by doing well on trips such as these, and if I had got a decent opportunity and been good enough to take it there is always the possibility that it would have been noted in high places. As it was, Johnny Gleeson of Australia was used as the main spin-bowler, with Brian Close coming on himself if support was needed in that department. My role on the tour quickly became clear: I was to be resident twelfth man, captain's valet and social secretary.

It all gave me a good opportunity to get a first-hand view of Brian Close. I had heard all the stories of his indestructability and of his total confidence in his own infallibility, and now found that they were true. There was the time when he was fielding very close at silly point and a glancing blow off his temple carried to cover where the catch was completed. When asked later what would have happened if the ball had struck him between the eyes he is reported to have replied, 'It would have been caught at mid-off.' Whether that is true or not I do not know, but if it is not it should be, because in one match he asked me to field at forward short leg when he was at short square. His instructions were 'Be ready for rebounds.'

I had heard plenty of stories about his driving ability, so made very sure that I acted as his chauffeur rather than letting him anywhere near the wheel of the car. There must be something about playing for Somerset which affects handling a motor car. I once — and only once — accepted a lift from Ian Botham in his high-performance machine. It not only has a set of dials and instruments on the dashboard to rival Concorde, he drives it at much the same speed.

What I had not heard about Closey was his potential as world heavyweight boxing champion. He soon put me right. We were driving to the next venue on one trip when news came over the radio that Muhammad Ali had retained his title by stopping Dutchman Rudi Lubbers in the twelfth round of their fight in Jakarta. 'You know, I think I could beat him,' said Close, nodding towards the radio. I thought at first he meant the newsreader, but then it became clear that in a considered, confident way he was casually imparting that he felt he had a chance of beating the man reckoned to be the greatest heavyweight champion the world has ever seen. 'He wouldn't knock me out,' he said, 'and you never know, I might just get a lucky punch in and that's all it would need — just one lucky punch.' He really did believe that it might go that way as well, despite the fact that his boxing career had been confined to a few bouts in the army. There were times when Closey could make Walter Mitty appear a modest realist.

His belief in himself was so total that even had he ever got into the ring with Ali, and the Greatest (Muhammad not Brian!) had happened to be stung by some exotic insect causing him to fall to the canvas, the victim of some previously unknown allergy, Closey would have believed that it was all down to his efforts. When we were playing against Western Province in Cape Town they had lost an early wicket before Goldstein and Ackerman came together in a century stand for the second wicket. Ackerman was one of the hardest hitters of a cricket ball I have ever come across, and on this occasion Goldstein was not very far short of him. The opening attack had been torn to shreds when the skipper decided to give himself a bowl. His first ball, had it been any better, would have been dreadful. It bounced nearer the bowler than the batsman and was going down the leg-side. Goldstein wound up and cracked it towards square leg with incredible power. After leaving the bat it never rose or fell in its trajectory, or so it seemed, and might have killed someone in the crowd had not John Shepherd put out his hands and held onto the catch. As the fielders gathered round the bowler, Closey was flicking his fingers and saying, 'It's wonderful how this warm climate loosens up the joints', as if he had meant it to happen the way it did.

I am not sure whether he blamed the climate for his fingers getting too loose as Ackerman went on to hit 179 not out, with the captain's figures reading 11–2–57–1, and that solitary wicket all due to John Shepherd. His effort in Cape Town was popular with the captain but was nothing to the reception he and Younis Ahmed received when we went to Soweto to play an African XI. It was the first time a touring team had played an official match against a coloured XI and some 40,000 people turned up to cram into the ground. Every one of us was well received, but Shepherd and Younis were given tumultuous welcomes.

All this time I was becoming more and more proficient as a twelfth man. When I started the tour I did what was normal during the drinks interval and carried out a tray of squash. I soon found that this was not what the skipper required. He went on and on about wanting a cup of tea, and suggested that I slipped one in the middle of the glasses especially for him. I did make sure he got his cup of tea the next time the opportunity arose, but it was not secreted away among the other drinks. Instead I took out a tray on which there was a bone china cup and saucer, teapot, jug of milk and bowl of sugar, and then I went to great pains to pour it out in the full public view! On more than one occasion I even took a lighted cigarette out to him so he could have a couple of drags in the middle of a session.

I can remember one of the Essex players who has had plenty of experience as a drinks waiter, John Lever, indulging in a bit of tomfoolery at Taunton. Robin Hobbs was leading Essex, and just as a Lever over was about to start the drinks came out. They were all straight orange juices, and a lot straighter than JK's approach for the first ball of the next over. He pretended that his had been laced with a drop or two of the falling-down water, and after some giggles and 'hics' at his mark he set out — not towards the stumps but in the direction of Robin at mid-wicket while looking at me with a glassy stare at mid-on. It was a virtuoso imitation of a stage drunk, and brought the house down.

I also had to make sure that when Closey was out, I had the necessary supplies awaiting him in the pavilion. That meant a lighted cigarette and a freshly brewed cup of tea with two sugars, stirred. The only problem was that the way he was batting on the tour, the kettle had to go on the moment he went in or else there was hardly time for it to boil. He was batting quite well, however, in the last of the matches against the South African XI in Johannesburg and had got 14 when he was given out leg-before to Eddie Barlow. He came into the changing room with the impact of a tornado. His face was like thunder, his bat flew in the general direction of the rest of his kit as he went to great length to explain that he was two inches outside the off stump

when the ball beat his forward stroke and hit the pad. 'I was just two inches outside, two inches,' he kept saying.

Later that evening there was a reception at which I, as social secretary, was responsible for the entertainment of our team. This meant making sure that there would be some beer available and arranging for some women on tap, or vice versa. It turned out to be a moderately tame evening with our boys doing their best to keep the small talk going and dancing with a motley array of local talent. All of a sudden, I was aware that the chatter was subsiding and all attention was turning to the doorway where stood a blonde whose appearance and proportions were capable of stopping any show. Comparing her to the other girls there in cricketing terms, she was Test class and they were clubbies. As such, she became the target for the skipper, who homed in with the accuracy of a heat-seeking missile. Out came all the charm as he introduced himself as Brian Close, captain of the English team, before he whisked her off into the middle of the throng.

It was a good hour later that I spotted the two of them, still drifting around the dance floor and deep in conversation. I decided to find out the secret of his line of chat. I managed to steer the carthorse I was dancing with towards Close and partner. He was holding his hand up with thumb and forefinger close together. Whatever approach he was using, I thought to myself, it was certainly not bragging. As we got closer I overheard the honeyed words he was pouring out, complete with hand actions, to this gorgeous creature he had cornered. He was saying in earnest tones, 'I was that much outside off stump, just two inches.' I can only think that he had as much success with her as I did with my bowling on that tour.

Closey often appeared to have trouble with the odd fraction of an inch here or there. There was another occasion when we were playing together for a D.H. Robins' XI, but this time at Harrogate. It was in 1974, when he was skippering Somerset and so took some delight in leading the Robins' XI against his former county, Yorkshire. Naturally he was keen to do well personally and was going quite well with the bat when he attempted one big hit too many. He had already taken advantage of the fairly short boundary when he was denied another six by a catch on the rope. 'I can't understand why it fell short' was his catchphrase of the moment. I held his bat in an ostentatious display of mock scientific study, looking at it from every angle, before holding it against another bat in such a way as to make it appear slightly narrower. In fact it probably was a fraction under the regulation width, but I played this up and offered it to Closey as an excuse for his dismissal. He seized it with alacrity. 'That must have been the problem,' he exclaimed. 'My bat's too narrow.' The fact that he had middled the ball but failed to time it properly did not seem to come into his calculations, and even had he planed an inch off either side it would have made not one jot of difference to the stroke which got him out!

CHAPTER FIVE

Tourist Class

Test players tell me that they never tire of the excitement building up to an official tour. Even the certainties like to tune in to the radio to hear their name read out and and then go through all the preparations before flying off to a place in the sun, playing cricket for their country during an English winter. I have never been fortunate enough to be included on such a list, but I have enjoyed a wide variety of tours to most parts of the globe. As far as I am concerned, all these trips have just one drawback — we always fly to the destination. To be exact, I have no fear of flying whatsoever; I am petrified of crashing. I share the sentiments of the American comedian who was asked if he had a good flight and replied that any flight you walk away from is a good one. I tend not so much to walk away from them as to stagger. Mine is not Dutch courage, but it originates in bottles from somewhere north of Berwick-on-Tweed.

That visit to South Africa with Derrick Robins' XI represented the first long flight I had ever been on. It took twelve hours to get there and in that time I had got drunk, sobered up, become scared and so got drunk again. It was not only the flight out there, either. We often moved from one fixture to another by air to cover the vast distances in time to get to the next game, but as I was unlikely to be playing when we got there I was not over-impressed by the necessity for speed.

That was especially the case when it involved landings like those at Border, to the north of Kimberley in Cape Province. I had found out that my room-mate, Peter Lee of Lancashire, was just about as magnificent a man in flying machines as I was, and so we spent flights playing cards. We had a game that did not involve too much concentration but just enough to distract us a little from the perils we envisaged every time we left terra firma. It was a version of snap.

On our second trip into Border we knew what to expect. The runway was only just long enough to take our plane, and the first landing there had been not so much a gentle approach as a plummet. Having made what I can only describe as a controlled crash, I then had visions of the pilot throwing out the anchors and putting his foot through the floor on the brake pedal in order to stop the infernal machine before he ran out of runway. He managed it with no more than 60 yards to spare, though with a more sophisticated means of arresting the plane's forward motion than I had in mind. Having experienced that once, the tension in our part of the cabin reached unhealthy levels. Gradually concentration moved away from the game and focused entirely on the aerial manoeuvres. My heartbeat was as one with the revolutions of the engines, beads of sweat were pulsing from my temples. It was only when we finally came to a halt that I realised Peter Lee and I were holding hands not of cards, but with one another!

My travels with Essex have involved quite a bit of flying, too. Fortunately not all the journeys have been as terrifying as one we had to Gibraltar. I believe that pilots find it a bit of a challenge landing at the Rock, because Spanish airspace restrictions mean that they have to go in over the sea, bank round, and then get down onto a runway built out into what is presumably the Atlantic on one side and the Mediterranean on the other. For me it was a case of being between the deep blue sea and the deep blue sea.

I always like to get an early view of the runway as we come into land. My heart has already gone leaping about all over the plane as the noise of the engines changes on the approach descent while I watch strange pieces of wing stick out and drop down. Then there is the clunk of the undercarriage going down — a sound that sends my pulse rate up in sympathy as I wonder whether it all might have dropped off completely. But then, once I get a glimpse of the runway below me, getting steadily and comfortingly closer, I start to calm down a little. Going into Gibraltar is not quite like that. As we banked I thought we were turning over through what used to be called a victory roll into a dive of death. Then I saw the runway, looking like a twelve-inch ruler balanced on somebody's finger. By the time our pilot had brought us skilfully down I was a nervous wreck, but as I realised we had made it, my relief engendered high elation and the other members of the team had to restrain me as I stood in the aisle belting out 'For he's a jolly good fellow' in the general direction of the pilot.

It is all fairly ironic that someone with such a view of flying should have married an air hostess. I met Barbara in Ireland when Essex took a mid-season break to play a two-day match against an Irish XI in Dublin and a one-day fixture against a team called the Leprechauns at Leinster. She had been watching the first day of the Dublin game with a friend connected with the Irish team, and I persuaded her to come along to a reception being held that evening at the British Embassy. Things developed until I decided the only way I could get her out from behind the wheel of her Mini, which she drove around like a maniac and on which she picked up parking tickets like some people collect stamps, was to marry her. That way I could get her to England and make sure that I did the driving.

Now you hear a lot of stories ridiculing the Irish, and I was quite prepared to believe them. I watched Barbara very carefully and in a way I was almost disappointed that she did not provide me with a fund of stories about the stupid things she did. I had almost come round to thinking that one idiot is enough for any family to endure when she at last came good. It was some years after we were married, and we were living near Colchester. We were due to go out with the Savilles, but arrived a little early to find Graham playing bingo with his two young daughters. Barbara and I joined in with a card each, and were given some counters to cover the numbers as they were called. Graham was pretty good at that job, chanting away with a nice patter until he was interrupted by Barbara saying, 'Could you not slow down a little? It's terrible hard lifting up all the little counters to see if I have the numbers.' Only an Irish girl could cover them all up first and then take the counters off as they were called!

On my many visits to Ireland it is not that sort of thing that has stood out, but the amazing hospitality. We have tried to reciprocate on the numerous occasions the Leprechauns have come back to play against us when they have included guest players like Julien Wiener and Kim Hughes of Australia. There was one occasion at Chelmsford when the lunchtime hospitality got so out of hand that when I bowled directly after the interval, I managed to deliver two overs without getting a single ball to pitch. It was hardly surprising as I was not absolutely sure where the other end was! Irish cricket, however, is of such a standard that they do not need to rely on ringers to give even a powerful English side a good match.

I can remember being one of about seven county professionals playing for Brigadier Norman Butler's Pioneers touring team against Clontarf. Having won the toss and elected to bat, we thought we were in for a nice restful day as New

Zealand Test opener John Parker went out to open our innings. In fact Mike Hendrick and I were so confident that we went down to the local. Some three-quarters of an hour later the Brigadier's Jaguar came screeching to a halt outside and he ran into the bar to tell us to get back as quickly as we could because we were needed to bat. When Mike and I got back to the ground we were 50 for 6 and went on to lose by six wickets.

It was on that trip that I first came across the Irish Jewish fraternity. They had some great characters among them, and none more so than a little fellow called Tony Leon. He had a passion for cricket bats, especially those used by first-class cricketers. If he saw a county player with a bat in his hand he would ask to try it, praise its weight and pick-up, and then put in an offer. The deal having been completed, he would take his new pride and joy for safe keeping to the boot of his car, and when he lifted the lid you would find he had more bats than Gray Nicolls! Even then he would ask for a couple more to be sent over to him, and the tragedy was that he never really enjoyed the talent which he hoped his collection would bring. Never mind, not all rare book collectors are great authors.

I have travelled around quite a bit with the Pioneers, including one memorable visit to Germany. Now Germany might not sound like a very likely place for a cricket tour but in fact the game is played extensively with a large contingent of British servicemen out there. The only problem associated with that is the price of drink. Not that it is too high: for £2 you could get paralytic, or I could. It was after such a visit to the mess that John Lever and I went out to a Berlin night-club on the eve of the first match of the tour. The Berlin night-life has to be experienced to be believed and we were not going to miss out. There we were, chatting up a couple of stunning creatures, dancing with them and generally getting on rather well, when they went off to attend to natural calls. We watched them go towards the cloakrooms, saw them smile back at us, and exchanged notes about being on a pair of winners. Our faces must have been a study a few seconds later when they disappeared through a door marked 'Herren'. As cricketers we should have been able to spot a wrong 'un.

I have been to Germany on several occasions on cricket tours and somehow never manage to get by there without some incident or another. Our former secretary at Essex, Ronnie Cox, used to run army cricket out there and the county have been on a couple of trips through the connection. This meant that I got to know some people quite well, and I was paying a social visit to a mess to look up some sergeant friends when I encountered trouble once again. They were involved in the running of an inter-unit hockey match and knew that years before, I had been a hockey umpire. They said they only had one and asked me to fill in. I made the usual protestations about having forgotten the rules, not having a whistle and having no kit, but all were to no avail.

It was only when I got out onto the pitch that I first realised there was no other umpire and I was on my own. On an all-weather pitch, where the ball moves about rather quicker than I could, I did my best to remember what constituted obstruction, the niceties of the reverse stick rule, and when a tackle from the left is permissible. In fact, I found that my umpiring had to be no more sophisticated than the play and that was little more than basic. I am sure some of them were good players, but they were not allowed to show neat stick-work because at the first sign of a skill they were hacked down by an opponent using his stick with all the subtle persuasion of a claymore. I decided that I had to make an example of someone and so the next time I noticed a crude tackle I called the offender over and began my lecture. He was not small, but he listened to my summing up and accepted

sentence, a temporary suspension, with commendable calm. It did not stop him repeating the offence when he came back onto the field. This time I showed him the red card and he spent the remainder of the match as a spectator. I thought I detected a certain chill in the atmosphere and it was not until half-time that anybody told me I had just sent off the visiting commanding officer. After the match a few players mentioned that they had enjoyed the game and thanked me for officiating, and then I noticed the banished colonel approaching. I was not quite sure what to expect, but it certainly was not a shaken hand, a warm smile, and the words, 'A little strict, I thought, but well done.'

Had I been in the army myself I think I might have got into a fair bit of trouble with officers, as I seemed to be able to rub them up the wrong way without really trying. On a Pioneers tour to Barbados I crossed paths with Brigadier Butler merely because of an injured shoulder. It prevented me from bowling properly and I mentioned this on the morning of a match against Pickwick on the Kensington Oval. It was a more than useful team for a crowd of clubbies plus a few pros to come up against on a holiday trip, for Geoff Greenidge, Alvin Greenidge, Emerson Trotman and a few other past and present Barbados players were in their line-up. Even so, the Brigadier said in crisp military tones that if I could not bowl I could not play. It took Graham Saville some time to explain that I would be a better bet for some runs than half the rest of the side before he relented. Such is the standard of club sides out there that even in friendly matches there is usually a quick bowler or two ready and able to whistle a few round your ears, whoever you are. I wondered just how grateful I should have been to Sav for talking me into the team when I saw what happened to Don Brennan. He had been keeping wicket immaculately on the tour and was always smartly turned out in his England sweater. Perhaps it was that sweater that incensed one of the local quickies who steamed in and felled him with a bouncer on the head. I wondered just what I was involved in when a 60-year-old no. 10 batsman was getting hit on the head.

Even friendship off the field does not stand in the way of West Indian quickies and their targets. Keith Fletcher was on tour in the Caribbean with England and came up against county colleague Keith Boyce appearing for the West Indies in a Test. In such circumstances Fletch would have been expecting Boycie to slip into top gear: what he did not expect was to be greeted by a fusillade of bouncers which threatened his tenure on life, let alone his wicket. The first four balls he received went whistling past his head at great pace. At the end of the over he went down the pitch and inquired of the umpire, Douglas Sang Hue, how many more bouncers would be required before it constituted intimidatory bowling. 'Bouncers?' beamed the umpire. 'Dem's not bouncers, man, dem's long hops!'

I encountered something similar myself in this country. John Price, the Middlesex and England opening bowler, used to spend his winters working for a sports goods firm and his business took him to Ipswich. I offered 'Sport', as he was known, accommodation and he spent a few days and a couple of very sociable evenings with us. It was very early in the next season that the fixture list took us to Lord's. At that time of year quick bowlers have not usually loosened up properly, and so it was with no great trepidation that I went out to face Price with the second new ball. The preliminaries to facing my first ball included an exchange of greetings with 'Sport', who thanked me profusely for putting him up. Niceties completed, he came pounding up the long curving run he used and whacked it in just short of a length. It was what we call a 'Harrier', after the vertical take-off fighter, and was still rising as it whipped smartly past the end of my nose. Bill

71

Alley was the umpire, and he asked me what I had done to upset 'Sport' because it was the fastest ball he had bowled all day.

Despite the fact that we were nestling in the tropics, the Pioneers' Barbados tour was plagued by rain. It would come in the morning, make play impossible for the day, and then clear up. The pros did not complain too loudly as we could enjoy the holiday, but for the clubbies it was all very disappointing as they were there essentially to play cricket. I was asked, or ordered, by the Brigadier to skipper the side for a match on the other side of the island against Windward Cricket Club. As we set off past the top hotels on the coast in the St James's district, the rain was lashing down and the prospects of play looked about as remote as we found Windward to be. Eventually we found the ground, and although admittedly it had stopped raining, everywhere was awash. I found a chap in a white coat and asked for confirmation that no play would be possible that day. He flashed a smile which was all teeth and gold fillings – he probably had more wealth in his mouth than I had in the bank – and imparted that while we would not start on time, we would start.

A lake next to the ground had burst its banks and flooded, and the wicket was not visible above the water. An hour later the sun had dried it out a little, but I was still flabbergasted when they came in to say that we would begin in half an hour and enquiring if I would like to toss. From the pavilion I could now see the green strip of the wicket, and I waded out there to toss. 'Waded' was the right word, for the water still lapped over my feet, and on reaching the pitch I found it consisted of grass cuttings laid down in the vicinity of the wicket, rolled and built up until it was above water level.

I won the toss, decided I was not going to field and run the danger of contracting swamp fever, so elected to bat. The big, brave Ray East told the rest of the side he would show them how to deal with a wet wicket and then watched as an even bigger West Indian marked out his run with every step sending up a splash of water. It is usually said of such bowlers that they charge in like enraged bulls. This one looked more like an evil shark as he rushed through the water with teeth glinting. He pitched the first ball short, I went onto the back foot to hook without having much idea of what the ball was going to do, and was in no position to play any sort of shot as it trundled along the ground. It was quite impossible to hit a four, and in our 30-over innings there was just one six when a full toss from a medium-pacer was middled. We were bowled out for 70 from the last of our allotted deliveries.

It was like some sort of dream, going out to field in what was little more than a lake with this island of grass cuttings in the middle. Telling someone to go and field in the deep took on an entirely new meaning — it meant that the water came up above the ankles. I was at mid-wicket and chased a ball which had sunk about ten yards away. As I reached it and put my hand down, a frog gave a croak and jumped over it. For somebody who shrinks away from any type of creepy-crawly this was a little disconcerting, and when suddenly hundreds of other frogs answered their mate's call and jumped about all around me, croaking their heads off, I made for the middle. Furthermore, I stayed there and sent others to field among the wildlife.

Strange as it might seem, we took the last Windward wicket off the last ball of their 30 overs with the scores level, and so it was a genuine tie. We left the opposition to their frogs and made our way back to base past the cove where the day's non-combatants had been enjoying the beach. It was not only the sun and the sand they had been enjoying, for after leaving the frogs behind we found a lot of newts: there was a little bar in the cove where the owner had devised a cocktail consisting of two parts dark rum, a shot of light rum,

a generous dose of Galiano, all topped up with fresh orange. It was called a Freddie Fudpucker, and after two or three of those the orders became quite disgusting.

Just to round off that tour we had a dreadful flight home. We lost an hour on schedule in the air alone as the 'plane was pitched and tossed in a tropical storm. I swear that at one time we were going backwards. Even the stewardesses were strapped into their seats, people were screaming and saying they wanted to get out, and I merely came close to passing out. Meanwhile Barbara, seven months pregnant, just sat serenely knitting and recounting tales of what she considered to be bad flights. 'This is nothing,' she kept on repeating. It was nothing short of purgatory.

That tour, which I thought was to be my last trip any-where, was my second visit to Barbados. I had been there the previous winter with Titchener-Barrett's English County XI on a three-week trip which took in Trinidad as well. It was a tour of constantly changing plans, for originally it had been scheduled as a tour of all the islands. Then Barry Wood was called out to New Zealand to join the England party as an opening batsman so it meant we needed an opener ourselves. I cannot remember whether I drew a short straw, was threat-ened with dire consequences by my team-mates if I did not do it, or actually volunteered for the job in a moment of total insanity, but I found myself going out to open the innings in Barbados against a telegraph pole who could bowl a bit quickly. I was not surprised a few years later when people started to talk about a fellow called Joel Garner. I had met him.

I was borrowing an Australian-style cap from the Northamptonshire wicket-keeper, George Sharp, and I am convinced that the 'Big Bird' thought I was an up-and-coming Australian opener. While Barry Wood had flown halfway around the world to get a first ball in New Zealand, I stayed in Barbados and got 30-odd for the touring side. Against Joel Garner I do not claim that I got onto the front foot and hammered him back straight, but the odd little nudge and tickle did the trick. I kept fairly permanently on the back foot when I came up against another budding quickie called Wayne Daniel. I thought he might develop usefully, for even then he could hurry it through just a little. At least it came straight on and did nothing extravagant off the pitch. I might not have done a Closey and allowed the ball to bounce off me rather than give my wicket away, but I did keep it out for a while.

That was not the case at Bristol some years ago when we were playing Gloucestershire on a pitch which gave the quicks a bit of a chance and when we came up against Mike Procter bowling at his fastest. For some reason he did not like Essex much and seemed to be able to pull out that little bit extra. It was perhaps no mere coincidence that he twice did the hat-trick against us. On this particular occasion we were trying to hold out for a draw on the last day when I was joined by David Acfield coming in at no. 11. As he came in, 'Ackers' walked up to me and made it perfectly plain that there might be half an hour to go, but that he did not expect to spend a single moment of it in the way of the set of stumps at which Procter was bowling. He bravely accepted responsibility at the other end, where John Mortimore was looping down some rather gentle off-breaks.

Knowing Ackers to be a man of resolute character when it matters, I realised he meant what he said and so had to face the next over of savage pace. Picking which shot to play was not the main problem; merely seeing the ball was enough. I waved goodbye to a couple as they sped past, and then found one lifting steeply off a length to my knuckles. I thought I had fended it off with a certain panache until Alistair Hignell went full-length at short leg to pull off a remarkable catch.

As I turned to leave I noticed that the umpire was signalling a no-ball. I called over my shoulder that I had had enough and that the silly sod should get his arm down before anyone saw it but it had been noticed and I had no alternative but to face the rest of the over. Procter was reasonably unpleased by events, and I found that if I could take care of my person, the stumps could take care of themselves. Next over, Ackers got bowled by one of those off-breaks at the other end and I headed for the pavilion before anyone changed their mind this time.

There was another occasion when I had to face a hostile barrage from Procter. We were playing on what is commonly known as a 'sporting' wicket at Cheltenham, and one ball from the South African actually flicked my nose as it went through. I jumped back and hastily probed my face for signs of a lost pint or two of blood. To be honest there was none when I examined the hand which had been checking for it, but I was still pretty shaken. The Pakistani Test player, Sadiq Mohammad, was fielding at short leg and came up to enquire about my health. I made a dismissive gesture and assured him that I was all right, but my hand just brushed him. This was the signal for what was, to be kind, an over-reaction from him. He went dancing around demanding an apology. Dicky Bird, the umpire, had seen exactly what had happened and got play going again, but Procter demonstrated quite clearly that he took Sadiq's side. I immediately received two short deliveries and the umpire intervened with an official warning to the effect that any more bouncers by Procter would result in his suspension from bowling in the innings. He resorted to bowling off-spinners off a two-yard run, though still managing to stand one up to an uncomfortable height. He was taken off at the end of the over and I went on to get a fifty. There was still a bit of atmosphere when a wicket fell and last man David Acfield came in. As he passed the covers Zaheer Abbas called out, 'Bring back Proc.' Recognising his own lack of batting potential, Ackers defused the situation with a haughty 'I can assure you that will not be necessary.'

I found batting much easier on another of my winters in the sun, this time in Zambia where I went with Warwickshire as a guest player. Many of the younger members of the Warwickshire staff were on that tour and I soon became known as 'Uncle'. I batted at no. 7 in the first match and got them out of trouble with an eighty, and from then on went in at no. 4 or no. 5 and justified it. It was a very enjoyable tour, not only because the bowlers managed to locate the middle of my bat with some regularity, but because it was well organised and administered. Just one thing spoiled it – the local beer. It was not that it tasted bad. On the contrary, it went down remarkably well. The problem was that neither I, nor it, knew when to stop. I had probably had a pint more than enough the night before a two-day game, and next morning I found a definite advantage in sitting on the toilet. I got to the ground, walked into the changing room, dropped my kit as I went and continued straight through to the toilet once again. After a little while the skipper, John Whitehouse, came to the door and I explained that I could not possibly play. I thought I had explained my predicament, but a few moments later he was back at his post to tell me that we were in the field. John Hopkins of Glamorgan and a few others were a little fragile too, but it was me who had to leave the field on average once every five minutes. Just what the local spectators thought I cannot imagine. Or perhaps they guessed, for it was one of them who later warned me to look for 'floaters' in the brew.

I made sure I looked out for floaters in anything I consumed when I visited India on a brief trip under another England captain, Mike Brearley. I had heard a story that on another trip to the sub-continent Derek Randall had been afflicted while on the golf course. In mid-swing he dived for the bushes and after a few moments he asked his playing partner for some loo paper. 'Don't be silly' was the reply, 'who carries loo paper on a golf course?' The question did not bring an immediate answer, only a rather plaintive plea, 'Has anyone got change for a hundred-rupee note?' This time Brearley took a team to Calcutta to celebrate the Bengal Cricket Association's Jubilee. It was just a ten-day sojourn in November, with a five-day game to mark the occasion. We travelled on Air India, an airline where hospitality far outstrips punctuality. 24 hours of my life were spent in the air or on the ground under their care, and by the time we arrived there was just three-quarters of a day left for practice and acclimatisation. It turned out that it was virtually an Indian Test 2nd XI we were playing against, and it was in their season. We were in no shape to face the likes of Madan Lal, the Armanaths, Venkataraghavan and Gaekwad, and after we had lost the toss they reached 380 for 2 on the first day. By the end of that day we were more than a little hot and totally shattered.

Considering the amount of fluid we had lost, the drinks we had that evening could count as being for medicinal reasons. Surrey's Alan Butcher took his medicine better than most and is a very funny man anyway in the normal run of things. On that evening he really excelled himself and concluded what had become a one-man show by surprising some of the affluent Indians in the hotel cocktail lounge with an impersonation of Rod Stewart. We considered it very accurate, they very alarming, as Alan went through all the actions as well as reproducing the gravelly voice. He was not so chirpy next day. It was in the first over of the following morning's play that he walked in from mid-wicket as Jack Simmons bowled. The ball was short, the batsman pulled and the ball appeared drawn to Alan Butcher's forehead as a pin to a

magnet. It clunked onto his skull and bounced many a yard, while poor 'Butch' collapsed like a felled tree. He had not seen it coming and we did not see him for the remainder of the match. I have had a few sore heads the morning after, but his must have been the daddy of them all.

Quite what Mike Brearley made of all this I am not sure. I found him a little distant and uninvolved in what was happening around him. Obviously he did not behave like that when it came to important matches, but ours was always destined to be a lost cause before the trip began. There was an occasion in 1981, however, when I managed to get Mike involved in a little bit of comic by-play. It was shortly before the Oval Test of that summer against the Australians and we were playing a county match at Northampton. Mike Brearley telephoned the hotel to tell Graham Gooch that he had not been selected for the England side, but Graham was not around. He asked if any other Essex players were there and I went to the telephone. The conversation went something like this:

'Hello, Ray East speaking.'

'Hello Raymond, Mike Brearley here. I was wondering if . . .'

'Oh Mike,' I interrupted, 'I didn't think it would ever happen to me. After all this time, trying and hoping that I would get the call, it comes at last. Do you know I had almost given up hope of ever playing for England? Now you've made all my wildest dreams come true. Just think of it – Ray East playing for England.'

'Well, no, it's not what I telephoned for,' he tried to put me off, but I went on, pretending to be oblivious to his interruption.

'You don't know what this means to me. I know I've been bowling fairly well and I thought I might just come up for consideration but then I've been disappointed so many times before. Thank you very, very much, Mike, I'd love to accept your offer.'

By this time Mike had caught on that I was playing him along and burst into laughter at the other end of the line. He eventually managed to get over the real purpose for his call, while I never did get the call that mattered.

CHAPTER SIX

The Roadies

As a professional cricketer I must have travelled hundreds of thousands of miles, but despite the trips around the world it seems as if I do most of those miles on the A12. People who watch the game often do not realise just how difficult a life we lead, for the cricket is the easy part. Getting to the ground for the match is what takes it out of us. The commentators on 'Test Match Special' who love setting one another obscure quiz questions might enjoy the following:

What is the difference between a racing driver and a cricketer?

The answer is somewhere in the region of 20,000 miles a year, with the cricketer coming out on top.

The travelling from one match to another, with the possible Sunday excursion for a John Player League match thrown in, is the killer. One day I am afraid it could be just that, for a long drive after an exhausting day in the field would not be advocated by the road safety people as a way of reducing accident statistics. The John Player League would not have been possible in the days before motorways unless the fixture planners had a better sense of geography in those days. Now they have the benefit of a computer to help them work out the complex pattern for the season, and while it might be terrific at knowing when to avoid Surrey playing at the Oval on the same day as Middlesex are at Lord's, and realising that Yorkshire are likely to get a big crowd if they play at Scarborough in the holiday season, nobody appears to have told the machine that there is not a motorway between Northampton and Scarborough. That was one of the memorable journeys we had to make in 1982 to fit a John Player League match into the middle of a Championship fixture. By the time we got there I was beginning to wonder whether we might qualify for a team prize in the British Rally Championship as well as four points for winning the match.

Another classic we had a few years ago came on the Sunday of a three-day fixture against Nottinghamshire at Trent Bridge. After play on Saturday we had to head off down the M1 back home to Chelmsford, before making the reverse journey on Sunday evening. Our opponents? Nottinghamshire. The two sides playing at Trent Bridge had to do a round trip of nearly 300 miles to play each other in another competition. I heard another story involving us and Middlesex. We were playing in a Championship fixture at Derby and had to go to Cardiff to play a Sunday match. Middlesex were playing Gloucestershire in Bristol and the fixture list for Sunday saw them travelling to Derbyshire. Their opening batsman at the time, Mike Smith, is reported to have suggested that they should have sent us a set of Middlesex sweaters and nipped over the Severn Bridge at Sunday lunchtime.

Then there was the journey I remember which proved to be one of the hardest I can have ever undertaken. We had spent the last day of a three-day game in the field at Colchester before packing our bags for the little hop over to Blackpool! That must be 250 miles as the crow flies; we had to do it by car over a cross-country route. It was early Saturday morning by the time we arrived and only a painfully few hours of sleep were available before starting a new match against Lancashire.

Guess who lost the toss and had to spend another full day in the field? Furthermore, the Sunday game was back at Old Trafford so we had to set off from Blackpool to Manchester, during the holiday season, and return that night. There is no way that we could be at our most alert and at the peak of fitness after a gruelling schedule like that.

American tourists are known for their 'This is Thursday so it must be Holland' attitude to travelling. I know how they feel, except that there have been times when mistakes have nearly occurred. At the end of one fixture in Leicester, John Lever and I were discussing travel arrangements for the following Saturday. 'Where are we?' I asked. 'Canterbury, I think' was his reply. We therefore fixed up to travel to Kent together, meeting in Chelmsford and using one car. It was only a chance remark from one of the others that put us right. We were not due to play in Canterbury at all, but Cardiff.

You need a mind like a railway timetable and an RAC Handbook to fit in all the travel arrangements properly. Some of our players seem to lack this. Alan Lilley did not get a degree in geography and it does show. There was one incident when he got very confused over the fact that he had to go to Northampton. It took a lot of explaining that Northampton was the town and Northamptonshire the county before he was confident of finding his way. It was only a few weeks later that we had to visit Hampshire and he innocently asked if Southampton was anywhere near Northampton. He is bad enough on English locations; overseas he becomes impossible. David Acfield was once recounting a story from his international fencing days. He said he was in Budapest when 'Lill' interrupted with what he considered to be an intelligent question. 'Was that in the Commonwealth Games?'

All this driving would be bad enough if we travelled in the

sort of luxury coach that even fourth division football clubs seem to take for granted. Compare those coaches – with their televisions, cocktail bars, spacious padded seats and little table lamps – with what used to be our normal mode of transport. The sponsored cars are fine, but if it was your turn to drive our old van, the last thing you felt like doing when you arrived at your destination was playing cricket. Now we have a new van offering some degree of comfort; there was nothing comfortable about the old one. It was a yellow beast of indeterminate age, but definitely venerable. It was of the type used by the GPO to go round mending telephones, and in fact it was rumoured to have seen many miles of active service in that very capacity before gravitating to us. It vibrated so much that after an hour at the wheel you felt as if you had spent a month working on a pneumatic drill. The noise matched the vibration, so it was advisable to wear ear-plugs if you wanted to avoid deafness for life. It also had the endearing feature of a petrol gauge which could, and often did, go from half-full to empty in a few yards.

This nearly got us into trouble one day when we were driving to Swansea to play Glamorgan. Graham Gooch was riding shotgun and I had drawn the short straw and had to drive the dreadful machine. We had rattled down the M4 towards the Severn Bridge when we had a dice with a lorry going up a hill. To anyone watching it must have looked like an action replay of some surrealist grand prix, such was our speed as we manoeuvred to find a bit of tail wind to nose us in front. Going over the brow of the hill I was in a good position, ready to make my decisive move by going into previously uncharted territory – the middle lane. We had got almost level with the front of the lorry and I was in danger of getting cramp in my right foot I was pressing the throttle so hard into the floor, when the engine died. Graham was yelling for me to stop messing around, or at least I think he was. I had to rely on lip-reading as the cotton wool stuffed into my ears against the noise of the van insulated me from his more obscene vocabulary. I looked down at the petrol gauge to see the needle resting firmly on the end-stop. I managed to ease onto the hard shoulder before we began the mile and a half walk to Aust Services with a can. As we were trudging back, England's opening batsman turned to me and, above the ebb and flow of the thundering traffic noise, said, 'It's a glamorous life we lead, isn't it?'

When, or if, we reach our destination the accommodation we have nowadays is usually pretty acceptable. We tend to stay in modern hotels which might lack something in character but are perfectly comfortable. In the old days, when money was tight, anywhere would do providing it was cheap. One of our administrators even came up with the idea that we should stay for a night in a service area on the M1. That was possibly the most unsatisfactory accommodation we have ever endured. Apart from the fact that there was traffic roaring past throughout the night, we had to go into the 24-hour cafeteria for breakfast: not exactly the surroundings in which you can wallow for a relaxed meal before playing cricket. It was while we were there that John Lever's blazer disappeared. He is convinced that to this day there is a lorry-driver plying back and forth from London to Leeds in full Essex regalia. JK got quite upset when we said it would be used to going straight up and down all day.

It might appear that county cricketers are always drinking. That impression is largely a false one, for while we might have a friendly glass on a regular basis, it seldom goes beyond that. Even so, accomodating us for an away match in a temperance hotel just because there was a good deal to be had was never a very good idea. It seemed like one to the secretary of the time, however, and so we were booked into this dry establishment in the Hagley Road when on a visit to Bir-

mingham to meet Warwickshire. I will always remember the sight of little Gordon Barker, whose figure made him look as if he was trying to smuggle two small boys in without paying everywhere he went, going to immense lengths to secrete four cans of beer about his person each evening. He did not find any bother in concealing the contents once he was in his room, despite numerous offers to help him dispose of the contraband.

That was not the last time a little tin plate ended up in an Essex player's bedroom. Another cheap deal in Wellingborough saw half of us in one hotel and the rest in another. The one I was in was pretty ancient, with lots of oak panelling, aspidistras and even suits of armour as decoration. I think it was Stuart Turner who came in one evening, got ready for bed, pulled back the covers and came face to face with a full suit of armour. Any of us might have got a little excited to see the contours of a figure awaiting us under the eiderdown after a long day in the field, but we would all probably settle for bowling to David Steele for another few hours rather than coming to terms with Sir Lancelot, complete with visor.

It was at the same hotel that Brian Taylor celebrated his birthday. He went out for the evening with friends, while we got to work 'redecorating' his room. To begin with, we stripped the bed of sheets, blankets and mattress so that all that was left was the metal frame. Then we collected all the potted plants we could find in the hotel and put them around the room before draping rolls of toilet paper across any spaces left in the portable jungle. We all waited up to hear the reaction and, as usual, Tonker did not let us down. He opened the door, switched on the light and, with a gasp, said for all the hotel to hear, 'What the hell have we got here then? Kew Gardens?' He had to find another room and pay a chambermaid to clear up, but he took it all in typical good heart and it was worth the whip-round we had just to hear that spontaneous remark to the world at large.

Sometimes our activities take on all the intellectual magnitude of a fourth-former on his first school expedition. Like the time we were in a rather smart cocktail lounge in Hove. It was always inhabited by a painfully precise member of the blue rinse brigade, complete with a disgustingly pampered poodle which could never have been called anything other than Fifi. John Lever, perhaps jealous of the attentions heaped upon the wretched animal, invested in a very lifelike plastic dog turd which he strategically positioned on the floor just behind Fifi. At a given moment we all began to sniff the air disapprovingly and with nods and nudges, to say nothing of a little throat-clearing, drew the attention of our Dowager Lady Just-so to Fifi's little indiscretion. To say she was horror-struck would be an understatement. If it was medically possible for anyone to die of embarrassment, she would have taken her leave of life there and then, only pausing to ensure that Fifi accompanied her on her journey to the next world. Amidst a veritable explosion of apologies and admonishments she removed the animal from the scene of the crime. We withdrew to watch her amazed expression when she returned to find a total absence of evidence.

Practical jokes like that are harmless enough in themselves, but they do tend to create a reputation. Even when little accidents occur it is assumed that 'those Essex idiots' have been up to their tricks again. There was a time when we were playing at Worcester and had the Sunday off. You would not think that we could have got into any type of scrape taking it easy, but you would be wrong. It was at the time Brian Taylor was captain and the South African, Lee Irvine, was playing for us. Lee was a great sleeper. For someone as alert and athletic as he was on a cricket field, he had an amazing capacity for falling asleep at any opportunity,

and he was not one to let an opportunity go by. After a lazy morning, a couple of lunchtime drinks, and with nothing that had to be done in the afternoon, there was only one place Lee was ever going to end up – on his bed.

Straight after lunch he was away to his room, crashed out on the bed, and one of the legs happened to break. In normal circumstances the captain would be informed, the cost of the damage would be settled with the bill, and the whole thing would pass over without untoward fuss. That is what would have happened if Lee had told Tonker, but nothing would induce him to do so. He was adamant that Tonker should know nothing in case he thought the broken bed had been the result of stupidity. Plan B was to exchange Lee's bed with a spare one from another room: a simple enough task in itself, providing there was a force of half a dozen men available, each of whom had served an apprenticeship with Pickford's. Bernard Cribbins once made a record which had a line something like 'Right, said Fred, all of us together, 1–2–3 and give a mighty heave'. We all tried together, pushing and pulling, shoving, lifting and straining. After immense efforts we had succeeded in getting the bed firmly wedged in the doorway. Most of us were in the room and therefore unable to get to the side where a gentle manoeuvre could have brought results, while the corridor was fast becoming full of people who had come along to find out what the commotion was about and stayed on to watch a virtuoso performance from a modern-day 'Crazy Gang'. Eventually, where foresight and planning failed, a little brute force sent the bed exploding out of the doorway like a champagne cork leaving a bottle. It was just a case of using the old engineer's maxim: if at first you don't succeed, use a bigger hammer.

We got the new bed in without as much difficulty, but our troubles had only just begun, for the damage had been spotted by an eagle-eyed chambermaid. When it came to paying the bill on departure Tonker, as was his wont, checked it all through. We were waiting for some sort of explosion, and it was not long in coming. On noticing the first rumblings of a very active volcano, everyone involved made their way as quietly as possible from the scene of imminent trouble. There was no escape in the long run, of course. Once he had regained his composure we had to suffer the inevitable lecture which started with one of his favourite catch-phrases: 'There I was, cap in hand, and nobody had told me a thing.' He scoffed at the very idea of it being an accident, and the hands had to go deep into shallow pockets for yet another whip-round.

The fact was that we were all in everything together, and while life with Essex might get a little childish at times, particularly in those days, it all helped to cement us as a team with a good team spirit. Most counties have cliques which become evident once play has ended for the day. They split up into little groups which seem to have nothing in common until they all wear the same sweaters at eleven o'clock the next morning. We have always been a close-knit team and the escapades and high jinks have all contributed. Ray Illingworth was once reported as saying, 'That load of madmen will never win anything until they learn some self-discipline.' He had it wrong. There could never be any disciplinary problems with a team skippered by Tonker, and it has never once happened that a light heart has interfered with hard-headed cricket sense. Our president, Tom Pearce, is always one of the first to remind us that we should play our damnedest but above all we should enjoy ourselves and play cricket as a game. It is a good philosophy, and when in 1979 it at last proved to be successful, it meant all the more because we proved to the more serious of our critics that we could win with a smile. We might be a bit mad at times, but the madness is in our lifestyle and not in our cricket.

CHAPTER SEVEN

An Everyday Story of Cricketing Folk

There is no doubt that I made the right decision when I turned in my electrical apprenticeship to become a professional cricketer. Now I cannot imagine any other sort of life. I have been lucky to play in such a friendly outfit, for we spend some five to six months each year travelling around the country, living and playing together. If you are with an unhappy and discordant side, life must be purgatory. It is a strange life, and its routine must be incomprehensible to someone used to getting up at seven o'clock every morning from Monday to Friday, catching the 8.15 train, arriving in the office by nine and then reversing the procedure in the evening. Compare that life to mine.

For many years now I have roomed with David Acfield. There was a time when John Lever came back from a tour with the idea that we should change room-mates on every trip to avoid cliques building up, and Essex tried it for a time. The feeling was that if you had the two spinners in the same room they would bemoan their fate at the end of the day together: 'Cannon-fodder is all we're good for.' 'Yes, they just use us to get the over-rate up.' That was the sort of exchange which might come about. As it is, there is little danger of serious rifts in our set-up, and so the musical chairs stopped and now I am back sharing with Ackers. There is no reason why we should get on well together, for he is public school and university, I am a country yokel. He goes bird-watching as a relaxation, I watch Ipswich play football.

Ackers is the organiser in the firm of Acfield and East. He is the one who arranges the call at eight o'clock with the newspapers, the *Sun* for me and his *Daily Telegraph*. He goes off to breakfast first, and I follow on a little later, taking him his *Telegraph* so that I can have my *Sun* back. After breakfast it is a question of making our way to the ground and there is the warm-up session on the outfield, with specific physical activities depending on whether a batsman or bowler is concerned. Then it is back into the pavilion for a cup of tea and, in my case, a cigarette. Nowadays I am the only smoker in the team. I did give it up for six months during the winter once, but as soon as I got back to cricket and the pressures increased I found myself reaching for the packet and that was that. I tried to tell the others that if we did not have at least one smoker in the side we would not be eligible for the Benson and Hedges Cup or the John Player League but they were not entirely convinced. Some of them still take their complimentary packets for wives or friends.

At the start of a three-day match one of the highlights of the day is the toss. The two skippers go out to the middle, they walk up and down the strip on which we are due to play and look at it knowledgeably. Then we see the glint of the coin going up and we all offer a little prayer that it will cease its spinning as our captain has forecast, since in that case, nine times out of ten, we shall bat and there is the chance of getting our feet up. We watch for signals from the pavilion and if we are indeed batting a variety of activities begins. The first three batsmen pad up and prepare themselves for the start, while I choose my spot from which to watch the game. Even nowadays I do not miss seeing too many balls being bowled. Some reach for their books and immerse themselves in a novel. There is always a clutch struggling with the *Telegraph* crossword and I help them, from my seat overlooking the ground, with the odd three-letter special. Brian Hardie specialises in the *Express* crossword, while most watch the Test match if there is one on television. Once again, I will do so only if I can see both the screen and the pitch.

John Lever's great activity when the innings opens is to go off in search of the physiotherapist's couch. It is not that he is a hypochondriac, but he finds the couch comfortable for a little nap. There was one occasion when we had a dreadful batting collapse and JK was needed to pad up. As scouts went around the ground to search for him, another wicket fell and David Acfield had to go in on one of his rare excursions from the no. 11 berth. JK was eventually found – stretched out on the physio's couch in the caravan used for travelling to grounds without their own facilities, and quite unaware of the drama outside. It is not through inattention that I am very often not ready to bat when a wicket falls. It is just that I am always slow getting pads on. I wait and wait and then rush around at the last minute with people buckling up straps, giving me gloves and sending me out, sometimes as the man just out is coming through the dressing room door. I think it must be a psychological block about going out to face the bowling.

After the match has begun, the next time we all get together is lunch. That is one area of life where I envy the businessman with his expense account banquets. We used to eat so many salads that there was a danger of contracting myxomatosis. Now there is some notice taken of requests for a cooked meal at lunchtime. I know these things have to be planned some time in advance, but it does seem uncanny how hot meals coincide with heatwaves. In general the food on the county circuit is unlikely to get Egon Ronay leaping about with excitement, except at Lord's. I am sure that the lady who is in charge of catering there, Nancy, should get a medal every time Middlesex win a title, for the opposition have a terrible habit of over-eating when they sample the delights of Nancy's kitchen.

Personally I do not have a large appetite at lunchtime and will only eat at all if we are batting. This is unlike John Lever, Stuart Turner and Brian Hardie, who have gargantuan capacities for food. I sometimes wonder whether JK got his England sweater for cricket or for eating! If we are batting and are not likely to be called upon immediately after lunch, one or two of us might wander round to the sponsors' tents or boxes just to show our faces and to help maintain their interest in supporting the club. This has become an important source of income in recent years and it does us no harm to help out with a little public relations work. If a firm has hired a marquee for the day and is entertaining a client, that client might enjoy his day a little more if he can go home and say that he has been chatting to England batsman Graham Gooch. It might just make the difference in swaying a deal, the firm who did the hiring thinks it all worthwhile, and so comes back again next year.

The team will be together again during the tea interval, when they gather round the sandwiches and cakes and devour them like locusts might a tropical harvest. It is at this point that the captain usually gives some clues about his idea of a declaration. When it comes, the opening bowlers go through an elaborate warming up routine in the dressing room, stretching and loosening all the muscles they are likely to need and a few more I do not think I even have. Knowing full well that there is no chance of getting on that evening, Ackers and I have our own routine. While the quicks grunt and groan we ever so slightly take the micky by exercising our spinning fingers, along with suitable sound effects of

immense physical effort.

Close of play sees us gathering in the sponsors' tent again, this time for a drink. Some counties mix well and we spend quite a bit of time with them, though seldom talking cricket for long. Others tend to keep to themselves and be less friendly. It is at this point that plans for spending the evening are formulated. Perhaps there will be a benefit function to attend. Cricketers do this for two motives. One is out of a sense of duty, because you will be helping a fellow professional and because it will be your turn or you have received support in the past. The other is hunger and the chance of a free meal and some entertainment for the evening.

Failing the organised dinner, we go out for a meal. With Stuart Turner and Brian Hardie I am one of what is termed the scum food eaters: we like to get something down our necks quickly. David East, John Lever and Derek Pringle are the curry men and two evenings seldom go by without them sampling the delights of the Orient, though there is nothing very delightful about the distinctive odour which pervades every corner of the pavilion next morning: it is hard to tell whether you are playing in Madras or Maidstone if you shut your eyes. David Acfield and Keith Fletcher invariably eat together because Ackers is the only man in county cricket with the patience to sit with Fletch while he finishes a meal. He plans each mouthful with the careful deliberation of a general working out the strategy for a military campaign. The fork moves in over the rim of the plate, makes straight for the meat, performs a flanking movement to pick off the vegetables one by one, before mopping up any outlying pockets of mustard or salt. Once the load has been safely lodged in beween the Fletcher molars, where it is remorselessly ground down, the whole circuit is performed again. It takes hours. I am sure his benefit dinners lasted longer than anyone else's merely because they could not start the speeches before he had finished his meal and by then it was closing time unless a generous bar extension had been arranged.

If we have been eating separately the various groups meet again for a nightcap back in the hotel and then turn in at around eleven o'clock. It is a lifestyle which might not appeal to some, and when we have just booked into our tenth hotel in the same chain but a different town in the space of three months, even I wonder what I am doing with my life. At the same time, it is this comradeship and happy spirit which is probably the first thing I shall miss when I stop playing the game full-time. The closeness of the cricket community can increase the pressures if a team gets near to winning something, or it can all become a long grind if you are finishing most matches in second place. Then the hotels seem awful, the roads are always busy, and the towns appear to have moved further apart. A few years of that and success, when and if it comes, tastes not just sweet but like undiluted nectar.

In 1979 triumph became a most welcome impostor for everyone who had suffered through less successful years as either players or followers of Essex cricket. It was the year in which cricket's perpetual bridesmaids eventually got married. Very often in the past we had gone very close. Always we had lost out to some intricate regulation apparently formulated to ensure we would not win, or we had brought it about ourselves with an attack of what became known in Essex as 'Augustitis'. We lost count of the number of times we worked ourselves into promising positions to win one of the major titles in May, June and July, only to fritter it all away in the closing stages. To an extent our lack of success resulted from a reaction to pressure, but if fortune plays any part in this game we were convinced that Lady Luck always took her holiday in August.

Having struggled through those barren years with hardly

any absence from the side through injury, it was ironic that I should miss the first exchanges of the season because of a groin ailment, which in the end our physiotherapist at Essex, Ray Cole, had to refer to a consultant. Ray Cole's arrival with Essex was the result of Keith Fletcher's insistence when he took over the captaincy. He realised that it was a false economy for a sporting organisation not to have a mechanic to keep its engines running on all cylinders. In my early days with the county we had a masseur called Harold Dalton, but he spent all his time looking after Trevor Bailey. Not surprisingly, Brian Taylor was not a fanatical supporter of full-time medical men. He often expounded his philosophy on physiotherapy: 'Good players don't need it, bad players aren't worth it.' That was the end of the argument for him, but Ray Cole has played a significant part in getting the team out onto the field in the right condition to play a match. He performed the same function with Colchester United football club, although he probably spent more of his time with them on repairs rather than tuning. I have heard a story that one such emergency repair brought Ray a considerable amount of embarrassment. One of the Colchester players went down with a bad leg injury and Ray dashed out onto the field to administer his medical expertise. He hurriedly strapped and bandaged the injured leg, but it was not until he went to collect his implements together that he realised he had formed a strong and binding attachment to the player – he had bandaged his tie to the limb.

Much of the team's fitness depends on the work which is done before the season starts. Players report back in various stages of physical decay, varying from those who have been away on tour and so are still fit to those who have spent the winter on activities such as attending dinners and watching television. Some have done a couple of evenings a week of squash or running once they have realised what a state they have got into, while the youngsters tend to be naturally fit. It was one of those youngsters, Neil Foster, who really showed up us old lags on a pre-season run. At the start of a three-mile circuit round the park at the back of the Chelmsford ground, those of us who do not happily fit into the 'natural athlete' category were in agony – not physical agony but the agony associated with deciding which muscle to pull first. Foster went off at such a rate that he quickly earned himself the nickname 'Brendan' and was back having a shower by the time the rest of us staggered over the threshold of the pavilion. Next morning he was off again like a stag and did not find himself exactly overwhelmed by sympathy when he genuinely did pull a muscle. As usual, David Acfield summed it all up in a most superior way: 'It's no good being able to run like a hare if you can't bowl' was his response. Keith Pont, who is not one to be left out of a situation like that, suggested that if any opposing batsman hit the ball three miles, we would be faster than any other county at getting it back.

Even with qualified medical attention at hand, it is usually the player himself who decides whether he is fit to play or not. The last-minute fitness test has come into cricketers' vocabularies whereas it was once a footballer's prerogative. I think it was Bob Wilson, delivering a piece of information straight from the teleprinter in Football Focus on BBC Television's 'Grandstand', who uttered those immortal words: '. . . and news just in from Old Trafford – Joe Jordan has pissed a fatness test.' I can remember once watching Brian Edmeades undergoing a late fitness test at Swansea. It was in 1975, when Glamorgan had a fiery fast bowler by the name of Gregory Armstrong. He had come from the West Indies as the new Wes Hall and Charlie Griffith rolled into one. He could probably match them for pace, but at the same time matched a paint spray for control. That did not matter too

much for opposing batsmen, but he also had trouble with his run. Just as he never bowled the ball in the same place twice, so he never seemed to run up the same number of paces for consecutive deliveries. This meant that one ball would be delivered at great pace from somewhere beyond the umpire's left shoulder, while you were afraid to play forward to the next one in case he trod on your toe, so far did he overstep the crease. At Ebbw Vale in a John Player League match he was bowling like the wind off 15 paces when he delivered a ball to John Lever which slipped out of his hand and rolled gently along the ground. John looked at me, batting at the other end, as if to say 'Shall I hit it for four and risk annoying him, or let it go?' He hit it to the boundary but did not get a bouncer next ball as he feared. Instead, he found hurtling towards his head a beamer which he just managed to fend off with his glove.

The thing about Greg Armstrong was that you never knew whether it was an accident or whether he meant it. Usually it was the former as he was a mild-mannered man, but that only made it more frightening to face him because you could never predict what was to come next. I never fancied batting against him, which was why I had more than a passing interest in how Edmeades fared in his fitness test at Swansea that day: if he failed and could not play, I was due to open the batting. I was not over-pleased, therefore, when I saw Robin Hobbs roll the ball along the ground towards Brian Edmeades, who bent down to pick it up, clutched his back and said he was unfit. Fortunately the Welsh heavens cried tears of sympathy for him and rain almost washed out the match completely. I did not get to the wicket until the third day by which, ironically enough, Armstrong himself was not fit to bowl. I found opening quite a comfortable experience against the medium pace of Malcolm Nash and Lawrence Williams in amassing an undefeated seven.

Strangely enough, my first real contribution to the 1979 County Championship success was as a batsman, though not an opening one. After recovering from my muscle spasms, I returned to the side against Warwickshire at Edgbaston. My 13 overs in their first innings had not brought a wicket, but at the end of the first day, when Mike McEvoy fell lbw to Perryman, I went in at no. 3 as night-watchman. I survived that evening and was not out next day until one short of my fifty, and then went on to take four wickets in their second innings. We won by an innings. As we already had four Championship victories to our credit at that stage I cannot claim that my return signalled a dramatic change in our fortunes, but it was reassuring to show I was still worth a place in the team on my return.

I performed the same role of night-watchman in our next match against Somerset at Bath. Again Mike McEvoy was dismissed just before the close and out I went to the middle. Again I survived and next day went on to 70, just one fewer than top-scorer Ken McEwan. In fact I have only failed as a night-watchman two or three times in my career since first doing the job against Somerset some years ago. I played it the same way as I did batting at my usual no. 9 position, even at Leyton against a Somerset side including Tom Cartwright. There was just one over left that evening so I went in to face Cartwright and hit him for three fours with gay abandon. I was equally uninhibited the next day with my job done and went on to 40-odd. Even my 12 in an over cannot compete with what may be the most irresponsible innings ever played by somebody going in to prevent the loss of a valued wicket before close of play. That dishonour must surely belong to Robin Marlar of Sussex, who once went in as a night-watchman and was out, stumped second ball for 6!

At this stage of the season I was more use to the side as a batsman than as a bowler because John Lever was out on his own in that department. Spurred on by his omission from England's Prudential Cup squad, he was rolling everybody over. He took no fewer than 53 first-class wickets during June, so there were not too many fish left for the likes of me to hook. Never mind, I still had my place at no. 3 in the batting order to occupy me! When the historians look back at the summer of 1979 I am sure they will be totally bemused by the fact that Ray East appeared at no. 3 for four matches in succession. The last of these matches was against Kent at Tunbridge Wells. Chris Tavaré hammered everything to the boundary in an innings of 150 and once again we lost an early wicket. I was therefore not out overnight when the rain began. Derek Underwood had taken the one wicket to fall the previous day and the thought of facing him on a wet wicket was not a comforting one for a side with its sights set on the Championship, especially as Kent were one of the teams in the challenging group. Normally we do not enjoy a match settled by the weather, but in the face of 'Deadly' Derek Underwood we were quite happy to see it pour for the next two days. Several choruses of 'Singing in the Rain' could be heard coming from our dressing room.

Our next venue was Southend, where we encountered our first turning wicket of the season. The first match there against Sussex gave no hint of it. We won by ten wickets and I bowled just seven overs in the match without taking a wicket. In the next match, against Nottinghamshire, it looked as if Augustitis had set in a little early. We trailed by 60 runs on the first innings, hardly improved in the second, and Nottinghamshire were left needing 170 for victory. At 87 for 1 their chances of achieving victory looked rather better than ours. David Acfield and I were in partnership and suddenly hit one of those wonderful patches when nothing can go wrong. One by one the Nottinghamshire batsmen were seen departing to the pavilion and Ackers and I had five of them apiece. The last nine wickets went down for just 28 runs and we experienced the never-diminishing thrill of being applauded off the field by our colleagues and crowd alike.

We were spending July at the seaside, for after Southend we went to Bournemouth to play Hampshire. This was the first time we had encountered their West Indian paceman, Malcolm Marshall, and the Hampshire boys told us later that it was the first time he had come across a really quick wicket since his arrival. He did not waste it. Neither did John Lever, who took seven wickets as Hampshire were dismissed for 128, but 80 runs on with seven down left us deep in the woods. I went in to join Brian Hardie when Marshall was rampant. Off the second ball of the one over I faced from him I was dropped at third slip by Nigel Cowley. I thanked him profusely but sarcastically, for I would have been quite happy to leave there and then. As it was, I prepared to face the next four balls of the over, each of which hummed through to the 'keeper. After the sixth ball had gone the way of the previous ones, I relaxed and started to make my way for a chat with my partner. I looked up to see Marshall at his mark ready to come in again and umpire David Constant holding him up until I was ready. I do not think I ever was ready for the seventh ball of that over.

If you have never experienced a missile travelling within inches of your face at great speed, you would not appreciate my feeling of relief as the umpire finally called 'over'. Now was the time and opportunity for a serious talk with 'Lager', as Brian Hardie is known to the team. I suggested that the only way I was likely to be either willing or able to stick around with him was for me to get to the other end and stay there. Stay there I did, watching Lager play a magnificent innings. He is always likely to improvise shots not in every textbook on batting, but he excelled himself against

Marshall's pace. Such was the pace of the ball coming on that he more than once went to hook and found the ball going on the off-side. He even 'hooked' a six over extra cover. Meanwhile I was plodding along and reached 48 before falling. We had put on 114 for the eighth wicket and when asked by a pressman what it was like in the middle, I replied that at one end I felt like Donald Bradman, at the other Donald Duck!

We won that one by an innings, and won again in the first match of Colchester week on what was termed an experimental pitch. A new type of marl had been applied in the hope that it would provide a hard, fast pitch as found overseas. It looked right and played wrong. By claiming the extra half-hour on the second day we won by four wickets after 36 of them had fallen. The second opponents on the 'beach' at Castle Park were Middlesex. The match began on 1 August and our old disease broke out. So did Wayne Daniel, who often seems to save a bit extra for us. We were quickly in trouble and just scraped past the 100 mark, before Middlesex moved past our total with just two wickets down. It was approaching stalemate, for they were not scoring very quickly, so Keith Fletcher decided to force the issue. He came on to bowl his rarely seen leg-breaks and picked up five wickets. It was a brave attempt to force a win, but we lost the match, and the next one at Worcester, by nine wickets and an innings respectively.

It was also at Worcester, but in 1982, that I gave umpire Fred Goodall his first taste of the way we like to play our cricket. He was over from New Zealand for the summer and was standing at the end from which I was bowling to Worcestershire's New Zealand Test batsman, Glenn Turner. Glenn had 95, was going well and was the one serious obstacle in our path to victory. He padded up to a delivery of mine which did not turn and I deafened Fred with what I thought to be a pretty fair shout. Fred was unimpressed by my appeal, and totally dumbfounded when I went back to my mark singing the old Beatles number, 'You'll get by with a little help from your friends'. Fortunately he had a ready sense of humour and we had a good laugh about it in the bar that evening.

There was another occasion when I was bowling and the cricket became a little musical. Derek Randall was the batsman this time, and he always fidgets around the crease, goes for a walk between deliveries and talks to himself. On this day he went further and began whistling quite loudly. I countered by beginning a tune of my own, so we had the ridiculous situation of me running up to bowl whistling, 'Arkle' whistling to himself as he settled into his stance, and general laughter from everyone else within earshot. It was quite a cacophony.

Derek Randall made his Championship debut against us at Newark in 1972, scoring a typical 78 littered with sixes and fours. His skipper that day was Brian Bolus, who strangely enough also scored 78. My recollection of that innings is of Bolus using his pads rather more than his bat, to the extent that I wondered if he should not be playing for Nottingham Forest instead of Nottinghamshire. At one stage of their partnership Randall hit the ball many a mile out of the small Newark ground. A different ball was selected by the umpire who offered it to the two captains for inspection. Tonker Taylor accepted it immediately, but Bolus was not so sure. He took it from Dicky Bird, looked at it closely and then threw it against his front pad. Only after it had proved incapable of penetrating that did he agree to play against it.

The shape of the 1979 fixture list meant sitting it out for eleven days before beginning the next match at Northampton. Stuart Turner took five wickets as we got them out for 224 before we collapsed from 118 for 1 to 199 all out. How long did August have to run? However far it was, Stuart

Turner would go all the way and he picked up another five wickets in the second innings. Brian Hardie completed a century and made the winning hit and we made for the pavilion to listen to what was happening at Derby: Worcestershire were there and a win for them would have left a mathematical chance of catching us. Peter Edwards, our secretary, made telephone calls enough to put the Post Office into profit for the year before triumphantly announcing a draw at Derby and the Championship for us. We did not know at the time that there had been some controversy at Derby and Worcestershire were far from happy about the circumstances of the draw, but we did not concern ourselves with anything as we sipped the warm champagne found in the boot of Peter Edwards' car and lived out every professional cricketer's dream – life as county champions.

CHAPTER EIGHT

One-Day Wonders

Northampton is not the perfect setting for wild hysteria on the final day of a county match. There had not been a massive crowd and most had gone home before the Derby result came through. The moment of victory was not acclaimed as had been our Benson and Hedges Cup Final success exactly a month before. The contrast between the scenes at our Championship triumph and a full house at Lord's after a magnificent match with an exciting finish was stark. I reckon I have had a bit of misfortune in missing out on some of cricket's major occasions, but I also know that I was lucky to be involved in that one and that others, notably David Acfield, could justifiably cast envious glances in my direction. He had played in all the zonal matches and had done a splendid job in taking important wickets and averaging something just under three runs an over. Despite those figures I came back for the quarter-final at Chelmsford against Warwickshire, which we won without undue effort. The same side was chosen for the semi-final against Yorkshire, where victory came again, but this time only after much tension and a few incidents which did not quite go according to plan.

To begin with, we won the toss yet it very nearly proved to be one of those tosses which it is as well to lose. The Chelmsford pitch tends to do a bit early on to help the seamers and on an overcast morning, when there was a hint of moisture in the atmosphere, it was an obvious insertion job, especially as Yorkshire had a fair hand of seamers themselves. However, after the sun had come through moments before the start of play, batting conditions became perfect and Yorkshire's openers reached 100 without loss shortly before lunch. The decision to put them in was looking less inspired, and it was easy to pick out Keith Fletcher in the field – he was the one with the red face.

Lever, Phillip, Turner and Pont had all had a go, but Lumb and Hampshire were going like trains with Lord's their only destination. It was at this point that I was summoned up to bowl. My first over confirmed the worst fears of the spectators and me, for it was merrily despatched by John Hampshire for a quick seven. In the next over I threw it up a little more and Hampshire responded by lofting me to mid-wicket where Stuart Turner did the rest. Nobby Phillip got rid of Kevin Sharp at the other end and Bill Athey was the next batsman. After a couple of generously flighted deliveries, I pushed one through a shade faster. Certainly it was a shade faster than his stroke and he was bowled. At lunch Yorkshire were 114 for 3, whereas a few minutes earlier they were looking at 120 without loss. Such a score would have represented a tasty aperitif with generous helpings of sweet to come, but the fall of wickets made lunch all too indigestible to Yorkshire systems.

Our target was eventually 174 for a place in a Lord's final for the first time. Yorkshire bowled well and fielded better, but nothing contributed more to our batsmen's downfall than the nervous tension which was forcing them into involuntary actions with the bat. Slowly the runs were added and we would relax, then a wicket would fall and nerves were jangling like fire alarms. It got to the stage that five runs were needed with three wickets in hand and nine balls to go. Stuart Turner and Neil Smith were batting, I was next in and Keith Fletcher was in the toilet. An instant superstition had developed whereby everybody had to stay exactly where they were. It had all the logic associated with stepping on cracks in the pavement but we were in no mood for logic. Fletch was in the toilet and there he had to stay. John Lever stood guard outside the door, Alan Lilley was watching from the balcony and relayed details about events in the middle. Fletch never did see Neil Smith hit the winning runs, but when he was let out after the event, he joined Stuart and me in behaving like any battle-hardened, experienced, unemotional professional sportsmen would: we sat down and cried our eyes out.

The night before the final itself we stayed in a London hotel and were offered sleeping tablets to help us relax. I decided to rely on the type of medication available in the bar, without indulging in an overdose. On the day itself I enjoyed an early breakfast and we were at Lord's by 9.15. It was then that the nerves began to make themselves known. I am not the sort of person you would expect to get anxious over making an appearance before a large crowd but this was something above and beyond anything I had experienced before. Even at that early hour the place seemed packed, and there was such an air of expectancy that it was as if you could reach out and actually touch the excitement in the air. To make matters worse, our followers were in far greater evidence than those of Surrey. People who had been watching us for years were there, we met families and friends, and there were former players everywhere we looked. We were suddenly hit by the responsibility we carried to fulfil all these good people's hopes. Failure was unthinkable, nerves inevitable.

Just going onto the outfield for some fielding practice

brought up great roars from the crowd. I had played in front of large and enthusiastic audiences before but this one made me freeze. I remember the first two high catches hit by one of our players who then called my name as the ball came down towards me. I didn't just drop them; I didn't touch them. I got into position without problem, just as on dozens of other occasions when we are going through such a routine before the start of play, but this time I just couldn't get my hands together. People thought that as usual I was mucking about, but not this time. My bowling action has been described as looking like a puppet with a drunken operator. Now I think a couple of strings had broken.

Nerves loosened as a stand from Graham Gooch and Ken McEwan put us into a position from which only we could snatch defeat from the jaws of victory. I tensed again when I came onto bowl, anxious to get the first over down to see how it was going. It felt good and I got a wicket early in my spell, so I settled down to enjoy the day. That serene mood lasted only until the closing stages, when the Surrey batsmen started to threaten our total. Then I tightened up again and I was grateful that it was Fletch and not me who found himself under the swirling skier that he clung onto at the end of Geoff Howarth's innings.

It took well over an hour to get changed, such were the celebrations and congratulations, but I shall never ever forget the feeling of standing with the cup and my mates on the balcony, looking out over a surging sea of upturned pink faces. I never could quite remember the rest of the evening. It was meant to be a quiet celebration dinner, and it might have been at one stage. It was just that it never stopped, and the celebrations of Saturday night merged into the preparations for Sunday's John Player League match at Colchester against Yorkshire.

That was a carnival for our supporters and an endurance test for 11 cricketers with hangovers of ridiculous proportions. We lost, predictably, and I cannot say we were desperately miserable about it. The pitch was a seamer's paradise, offering both movement and lift, so I confused the issue by taking 5 for 20 in my eight-over spell. Such defeats mattered little at that time for we had won something at last. Furthermore, we nearly won the Benson and Hedges Cup again the following year, reaching the final only to lose to Northamptonshire in a match in which I hardly featured. Every time I was due to bowl, Keith Pont took a wicket, so I did not bowl and I did not get in to bat until the final over when I could only watch Nobby Phillip striking out vainly for victory.

We were on the brink of getting back to Lord's for a third time in three years in 1981. We had reached the semi-final when we had to play Derbyshire for the right to play in the first Nat West Trophy final and had made a bit of a mess of our innings in difficult conditions. The pitch was a vivid green on the first day and we were all out off the last ball of our 60 overs for 149. Bad light stopped play with Derbyshire 13 for 2, and when we resumed next day the pitch was different in both appearance and character. Perhaps it was something to do with conditions overhead. Despite more favourable batting conditions, they did not prosper and we came to a dramatic conclusion. Derbyshire needed one run off the final ball to bring the scores level and so go through by virtue of losing fewer wickets. Newman played the ball back to Nobby Phillip and set off for a single. Nobby picked up the ball, took aim and threw at the stumps. He missed. If he had scored a hit we would have gone through and he would probably have been named Man of the Match with top score on our side and three wickets, too. Such is the margin between triumph and disaster in this game.

We were all dreadfully upset in the dressing room, yet had to console Nobby who felt it worse than anybody. What made it particularly hard to bear was the fact that Barry Wood, the Derbyshire captain, was on the telephone just outside our door, describing the finish to a reporter. That was too much, so we started singing. The chorus gathered momentum and he had to hang up, while everybody else in the pavilion was left wondering why a team which had just suffered a sickening defeat were singing themselves stupid. Knowing glances and nodded heads soon came up with an explanation: 'It's Essex, you know – mad, the lot of them.'

I had had a little jest at Woody's expense when we were playing at Old Trafford during his days with Lancashire. He got hit by Norbert Phillip in a particularly painful part of his anatomy and doubled up, with suitable groans and gasps, in what I considered to be a rather ostentatious display of over-acting. Consequently, when the twelfth man appeared on the field to bring him a glass of water I met him at the edge of the square, supposedly to carry it to the injured batsman. Instead, I drank the water in one go, thanked the twelfth man profusely and went back to my position in the field. Woody was not highly amused, and was apparently damaged rather worse than I thought because he had to leave the field. It is funny how a player hit in the box never gets any sympathy from anyone on the field. It is usually the signal for plenty of laughter and ribald jokes. I must admit that I have indulged in them myself, making my way towards the scorers while the batsman tries to recover, and signalling 'one short'.

We had lost a Gillette tie on the same 'fewer wickets lost' ruling the previous year, and had been thwarted similarly at Taunton in the same competition a few years before that when we needed three off the last ball and Neil Smith was run out within inches of getting them. The same thing happened in a Gillette quarter-final against Surrey at Chelmsford. We needed two to win off the last over with one wicket in hand, after I had been involved in a mix-up over a run with Nobby Phillip. He could have won us the match, his run-out was my fault, and I accepted it. There was still every chance of salvaging a win, especially as John Lever managed a single off the second ball to level the scores. We had a conference and decided that we should not leave it to the very last ball to get the single still required as the Surrey fielders would really be on their toes then. Instead, we would run on the fifth ball, whatever happened. I hit that delivery straight to Roger Knight at mid-wicket and ran. John, for some reason, decided not to run and I was left stranded. The next morning the *East Anglian Daily Times* carried the headline: 'East loses nerve and game'. It was no later than 9.30 that morning when the telephone rang at home. 'Is that Ray East?' enquired a pleasant-enough sounding voice. After I had admitted it was, the tone of the caller changed and he let out a string of obscenities, into which was woven the accusation that I had thrown the match, that I was not fit to belong to the Essex team, and that my continued membership of the human race would be in doubt if he had anything to do with re-election. He then hung up.

I heard no more from him until 1982, when we were playing the Indian tourists at Chelmsford. I played the ball back to Madan Lal who picked it up and turned to go back to his mark. As he did, I pretended to tip-toe through for a run. Brian Hardie was the other batsman and he was just one short of his career-best. He set off for the run, Madan Lal turned round and threw down his wicket. Again I felt sick about it, especially this time as it had been a joke which had backfired. When I was back in the dressing room I apologised to 'Lager' and sat down to take my pads off. The telephone rang and I was told it was for me. Having established who it was talking to, the voice asked me if I remembered the Surrey game and then let off with another tirade of abuse. I must say he had a marvellous command of the darker areas of the English language, going on for a considerable length of time without repeating himself once. I would like to meet him to have a sensible chat, but I suppose the chances of him reading this book are a little remote as I gather he is not my greatest fan and I do not think he is likely to spend money on it as well as on telephone calls.

The John Player League, too, had been a source of disappointment over the years as we had finished in second place in 1971, 1976 and 1977. That first runners-up medal was the hardest one to take, for we lost the title by just 0.0037 of a run. That was the difference in scoring rate per over between ourselves and Worcestershire over the course of the whole season. We also felt a little hard done by since they finished level on points with us anyway. I can remember watching them play Warwickshire on television one Sunday while we were involved in a local benefit match. Warwickshire ended the season bottom of the table, and it was not surprising if that match was anything to go by. Worcestershire's West Indian Test batsman, Ron Headley, was one of the better drivers in the game at the time and there were the Warwickshire bowlers, pitching it right up on a half-volley length without either a mid-on or mid-off.

My annoyance had not died down over that incident a couple of months later. There was a presentation dinner at the Inn on the Park and I left my car at Chelmsford to go by train. It was a splendid do, or would have been had we had the trophy to show for it at the end. Somehow it just served to rub in the fact that we had missed first place on the winner's podium once again. All the way back on the train I saw again

Ron Headley creaming drives through those vacant gaps in the Warwickshire field and worked out that had just one of them been cut off it would have been enough to make us champions. Somewhere at the bottom of the river running behind the pavilion at Chelmsford there is a John Player League runners-up medal. I threw mine there when I got back to the car that evening.

To win would have meant a lot to me, hence my symbolic if futile gesture, but looking back I am sorry for the likes of Brian Taylor and Keith Boyce. Tonker did a wonderful job for Essex cricket and I am not sure he received full credit for it. Boycie went through a time when his performances were holding the team together and was sadly missed when he went through injury. He had always put the money he won in things like single-wicket tournaments into the players' general pool and all of us still regard him as a close friend. When we won the Benson and Hedges Cup a few of us paused when the celebrations in the dressing room were at their height and expressed the wish that Boycie could have been there with us.

His place in the side had been taken by Nobby Phillip and he featured prominently in our 1981 John Player League success. For those of us who had just missed the title three times, it was the one we really wanted to win. Nobby had not experienced those disappointments, but he had a point to prove after the tragedy of Derby by the time we got to the Oval for the last Sunday of the season, needing to win to make sure. A shower of rain at two o'clock meant a delayed start, and this in turn brought into play all the complicated regulations designed to cover this sort of occurrence. Apparently they were too complicated for the umpires, Bob Herman and Derek Shackleton, to understand because they told the players that our innings would end at tea, usually ten past four. Nobby hammered Robin Jackman for 18 in what he thought was the last over, and Stuart Turner was run out going for a suicidal single off the last ball. 184 in 38 overs would not have been a bad score, but it was by no means safe, and with Nobby going so well and wickets in hand, another over would have been more than welcome. Fletch met the umpires at the pavilion gate to put his case and a BBC radio commentator quoted chapter and verse to Bob Herman, who looked up the special regulations, conceded that a mistake had been made and went out again.

Up in the dressing room our next man, Derek Pringle, was standing in a jock-strap and nothing else. He had his kit thrown on him and went out to face the last over from Roger Knight. He was run out without scoring and I had to go in to watch Nobby continue his amazing assault. I did not see where the ball went, I just ducked out of the way of the flying ball and watched Nobby's face crease into an enormous flashing grin as it sailed towards the outer limits of the Oval. The last two landed in the pavilion and his 19 off that over put the game beyond Surrey's reach.

The final stages were played out in the most incredible light. A storm cloud, dark and pregnant, hung over the ground itself like a canopy while sunlight filtered in all around, particularly in shafts between the tall buildings on the Harleyford Road side. Looking into the sun presented quite a problem for fielding, and towards the end of the day I was out at deep mid-wicket with Keith Fletcher on the square-leg boundary. We saw the batsman play a sweep and knew it was probably coming our way, but could not see the ball at all. It had nearly hit Fletch on the foot before he spotted it.

There followed the usual scenes of the crowd swarming onto the field as the last ball was bowled, the charge for the sanctuary of the pavilion and more celebrations. Another balcony, another trophy, more cheering, chanting, happy fans. For someone who had waited so long to take any of the game's honours, either as an individual or as part of a team, this was intoxicating stuff. It is at times like those that you experience a feeling of relief and achievement; it is after times like those that you have to set out on another season trying to emulate the previous one. We also had to answer the question which was always asked: 'Will success spoil Essex?'

The answer was an emphatic 'No.' How could we change the behaviour of a man like Keith Pont? He was contributing to the humour of the side within his first few appearances in the first team. That was back in 1970, when we were playing Derbyshire up at Burton-on-Trent. Somehow Tonker had managed to put Keith at third man one end and fine leg the other, so he had to break into a gallop in order to get into position in time. Naturally we took the opportunity to rib him with cries of 'Come on, son, you'll have to move quicker than that if you want to be a professional cricketer' and the like. Keith soon got his own back. As we changed places at the end of an over we heard a ding-a-ling coming from the boundary. There was 'Ponty', pedalling away for all he was worth on a bicycle borrowed from a boy in the crowd!

John Lever and I soon dispelled any danger that we might get too serious about life just after we had achieved our Championship success in 1979. Our last away match of the season was at Scarborough, and on our way from the hotel to the ground we stopped off at a seaside gift shop. John bought a water pistol which he later took out into the middle while batting and gave stand-in wicket-keeper Bill Athey a quick squirt as the bowler was running up. We also purchased a bucket and spade each, along with some swimming bands and a couple of kiss-me-quick hats. When we arrived at the

Postscript

Since this book first appeared in 1983 I have played another season of cricket, marked by more than its fair share of incident. We managed to etch our names indelibly on the roll of great cricketing disasters by losing the Benson and Hedges Cup final against Middlesex at Lord's when only victory seemed possible. We had lost a NatWest tie only four days earlier against Kent, and the odds of repeating such a debacle were unthinkable. We proceeded to do it to exactly the same recipe, only at Lord's there was even greater exposure to ridicule. I cannot claim that anything could compensate for that, but we did make amends by winning what is, for the player, the greatest prize of all – the County Championship. It was all quite in character, for Middlesex were the odds-on favourites but we kept going, they slipped up and we got in to pick up the pot.

Such a moment is one to be savoured, and I decided that it was also an opportune moment to conclude my career as a full-time player. I shall still be on hand should the need occur, but now my main activities will centre on coaching and captaining the Second XI. I have also taken another step into my past by going back to my old home village of East Bergholt to run a pub. I might have missed out on the three lions of England on my cricket sweater, but there can be no doubts about my qualifications to adopt the Red Lion as my livery!

ground the Yorkshire players were already out practising. Complete with our latest acquisitions, we made our way to the back of the public seats and started to barrack the players in front of the very serious Scarborough crowd, who took us to be loud-mouthed tourists. The players were getting more and more annoyed and it was a long time before they realised who it was making all the commotion. When they did, their practice collapsed in general merriment. Perhaps I have been wasting my time all these years waiting for the England selectors to call: maybe I should have got on the telephone myself to ask Bertram Mills if he had a vacancy for a clown.